JUNG
FOR BEGINNERS™

Writers and Readers Publishing, Inc.
P.O. Box 461, Village Station
New York, NY 10014

Writers and Readers Limited
PO Box 29522
London N1 8FB
e-mail: begin@ writersandreaders.com

A Writers and Readers Dokumentary Comic Book
Copyright © 1997
ISBN # 0-86316-184-7 Trade
3 4 5 6 7 8 9 0

Printed in Finland by WS Bookwell

Writers and Readers

publishing FOR BEGINNERS™ books continously since 1975

1975:Cuba •1976: Marx •1977: Lenin •1978: Nuclear Power •1979: Einstein •Freud •1980:
Mao •Trotsky •1981: Capitalism •1982: Darwin• Economics • French Revolution • Marx's
Kapital •Food •Ecology •1983: DNA•Ireland •1984: London •Peace •Medicine •Orwell•Reagan
• Nicaragua • Black History • 1985: Mark Diary • 1986: Zen • Psychiatry • Reich •
Socialism •Computers •Brecht •Elvis •1988: Architecture •Sex •JFK • Virginia Woolf• 1990:
Nietzsche•Plato • Malcom X•Judaism •1991: WWII•Erotica• African History •1992: Philosophy •
•Rainforests•Miles Davis •Islam• Pan Africanism •1993: Black Women • Arabs and Israel •1994:
Babies •Foucault •Heidegger •Hemingway•Classical Music •1995: Jazz •Jewish Holocaust •Health
Care •Domestic Violence •Sartre • United Nations •Black Holocaust •Black Panthers • Martial Arts
•History of Clowns •1996: Opera •Biology •Saussure •UNICEF •Kierkegaard •Addiction & Recovery
•I Ching • Buddha •Derrida •Chomsky • McLuhan •Jung •1997: Lacan •Shakespeare • Structuralism
•Che •1998:Fanon • Adler • Cinema • The Body • English Language • Postmodernism • Stanislavski
• Marilyn

DEDICATION

TO MY STUDENTS AND TEACHERS

CONTENTS

Jung, The Life

Jung, The Work

Appendix

JUNG
FOR BEGINNERS™

WRITTEN BY JON PLATANIA, PhD
ILLUSTRATED BY JOE LEE

Writers and Readers

The influence of **Carl Gustav Jung** has never been greater than it is today. "Introversion" and "Extroversion" have become standard words. Most people are aware of the connection between the "individual psyche" and the "collective unconscious." Many of us have secretly wondered about our own "complex neurosis." The influence of the darker "shadow" side of life is the subject of concern as we seek to understand the apparent inhumanity of our species. All of this and more has come to us through the voice of C.G. Jung who, perhaps more than any other single individual, has shown that psychology and religion can not only coexist peacefully together, but that they can enhance, inspire, and perhaps even complete each other — and in the process, help us complete ourselves.

Despite his monumental accomplishments, to this day Jung is still a controversial figure, variously referred to as a "philanderer" who slept with his female patients, as an opportunist who "squandered his wife's fortune," or as a thin-skinned "narcissist" who couldn't come to terms with the "negative father transference" he suffered in his break with Sigmund Freud. Many eminent ladies and gents regard him as something of a living saint, a modern prophet whose work on "Synchronicity" and human consciousness is on a level of originality and genius comparable to Einstein's contributions to quantum physics and big ugly bombs. And, far and away the most chilling, some people know and despise him as the "Nazi analyst of the Third Reich."

Strange as it may seem, they are all right.
Some people are so damned good that all we can do is look up to them.
Jung wasn't one of them.

He was a great man who made great mistakes.

JUNG: The Life

Mothers, Fathers, Saints and Sinners

arl Gustav Jung was born in Kesswil, Switzerland on July 26, 1875. He was the son of a Protestant minister, Johann Paul—who was, himself, the son of Professor Carl Gustav Jung, the elder. To say the least, C.G. Jung came from a family of deeply religious men. Jung's mother, Emilie Jung-Preiswerk was certainly a Christian—she was the wife and daughter of Protestant Evangelical ministers — but she was also something of a spiritualist. She thought about, saw, and spoke to ghostly figures from the dead. She straddled the narrow band that separates madness and hysteria from the purely psychic or mystical.

A few months after Jung's birth, his parents moved from Kesswil on Lake Constance to the parsonage of Laufen Castle above the Falls of the Rhine River.

My whole youth could be understood in terms of the concept of Mystery. Our family lived at the parsonage of the church and the church had a graveyard. The graveyard had sextons and the sextons dug deep black holes in the graveyard. Other strange men would come in black frock coats and lay the great black boxes they carried with them into the ground. Women would cry and lament.

My father would then proclaim that 'Lord Jesus had taken the deceased to Himself.'

I began to distrust Lord Jesus.

My father was a very bad advertisement for religion: He was unhappy, mopey, gloomy, depressed — real holy on the out side and just a heap of despair on the inside. As you can imagine, this was not particularly helpful for me when it came to my own identity development.

Now, mom, on the other hand, was somewhat hysterical and manic. She was also a genuine psychic. And she gave me a great deal of attention. That was lovely. I enjoyed it.

Unfortunately, my mother had to go off to some kind of sanitarium when I was a child. She was very loving but none too dependable.

And my father? He was too consumed by his own high-minded despair to bother with anything as ordinary as a child...

DOES GOD HEAR ME? IS THERE ANY SUCH THING AS GOODNESS? GRAND WORDS, BUT IN THE END WHAT DOES IT ALL MEAN?

Losing one's faith is not such a big deal these days, but when it happened to Papa Jung, it was as though the ground had opened beneath his feet, and there was nothing left to stand on. Carl would remember those days of the Reverend Jung moping about the place with no God to turn to. To young Carl, his father's idea of God was none too inviting anyway and offered little hope of consolation in this world. Religion for Jung became associated with a mixture of anti-Catholicism, fear, distrust, and death.

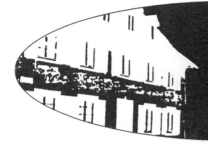

Enters the Basel Gymnasium.
Year: 1886
Age: 11

It was at this time that powerful dreams began to fill Jung's youthful world of mystery and the unknown. In later life, at the age of 75, he would recall the impact and importance of these early great dreams.

Through my childhood dreams I was introduced to the mystery of the earth....It was like an initiation into the darkness.

I am in the garden when I come upon a hole in the ground, a dark, rectangular hole, walled in stone.... I curiously peered down into it. Hesitantly, fearfully, I descended.... I pushed the curtain aside and there before me...on a king's throne was a huge thing...made of skin and naked and on the top was something like a rounded head with no face and no hair....On the top of the head was a single eye, gazing motionlessly upward.
CGJ

Although he could not have realized it at the time, Jung would dedicate much of his intellectual and personal life to understanding the meaning of symbols and dreams.

In 1895, Reverend Jung, who was getting no pleasure out of being alive, died. Jung's mother said to him that his father had "died in time for you" (a remark that can be interpreted in many ways).

I WAS NOT YET 20 YEARS OLD WHEN I AND MY MOTHER MOVED TO THE OLD BOTTINGER MILL.

The old Reverend's death had left his family nearly penniless, but thanks to the financial help of an uncle, young Carl was able to continue with his studies (on a very limited budget). Jung, like Freud before him, would have preferred a more research-centered life to a life actually practicing medicine. But in the end Jung would have to make a living. Money — or lack of it — contributed to his choice of attending the University of Basel where his grandfather had also graduated.

Boys, we havin' any fun yet?

Studies the natural sciences and then medicine at the University of Basel. Passes the state examinations.
Year: 1895
Age: 20

7

Jung's financial condition improved drastically when he married Emma Rauschenbach in 1903. Emma was "loaded." The marriage made it possible for Jung, age 28, to follow his desires and enter the emerging field of medical psychiatry.

WELL, FIRST WE HAD AGATHE IN 1904, THEN GRETTA, TWO YEARS LATER. FRANZ CAME ALONG IN 1908, AND MARIANNE IN 1910. THEN BEFORE WE KNEW IT, THE HORSE WAS OUT OF THE BARN, AND I HAD OUR LAST CHILD, HELENE, IN 1914.

TELL ME THE TRUTH NOW. DO YOU KNOW THAT I WROTE A BOOK? THAT'S RIGHT, BUT YOU NEVER HEAR OF ME, THE EMINENT EMMA RAUSCHENBACH JUNG—THE GIFTED PSYCHOTHERAPIST. THE FEMINIST. THE BRILLIANT AUTHOR. OF COURSE YOU DON'T!

ALL OF US WHO SHARED THE INTIMACIES OF CARL'S LIFE ALSO LIVED IN HIS SHADOW.

OUR LIVES WERE FOOTNOTES TO HIS OWN.

EMMA HAD HER OWN INTERESTS IN THE HOLY GRAIL.

MY CARL, HE WAS SUCH A LITTLE BOY AT TIMES. THEN AT OTHER TIMES, HE WAS OLDER THAN GOD. HE WAS DIFFICULT, MY CARL.

BUT, FOR ME, ON BALANCE IT WAS A GOOD LIFE AND A GOOD MARRIAGE.

AT HOME HE WAS A BUILDER AND A WORKER. JUST GIVE THE PROFESSOR A HAMMER AND CHISEL AND HE'LL SPEND THE DAY BANGING ON SOME ROCK.

BUT PLEASE MY DEAR FRIENDS, REMEMBER THAT MY CARL WAS A COMPLEX AND TROUBLED MAN. PERHAPS BECAUSE OF THIS—PERHAPS IN SPITE OF THIS—HE HAS LEFT US WITH A LEGACY OF THE HUMAN SOUL. I LIKE REFERRING TO THE PROFESSOR AS "MY CARL" BUT IT IS JUST NOT ENTIRELY TRUE, IS IT? NO, LIKE IT OR NOT, HE IS OUR CARL.

Jung's relationship to women largely defined the character of both his personal and professional life. As we have seen, his early interest in parapsychology was inspired by his mother. It was a maternal cousin, Helene Preiswerk, whose dissociated states provided Jung with the data for his doctoral dissertation, "On the Psychology and Pathology of So-Called Occult Phenomena," published in 1902 at the age of 27.

Helly, as his cousin was called, would later develop a positive transference to Jung. This "crush" of hers apparently led her to make up stories for the benefit of fascinating her cousin Carl.

Jung sometimes called Helly his "lost Jewish Princess." Which brings us to Vienna. . .

...WHEN IT COMES TO BEING JEWISH IN VIENNA, THE LESS SAID, THE BETTER.

...WHEN IT COMES TO *SEX* IN VIENNA, THE LESS SAID THE BETTER.

Jung, Freud, Intimacy and Betrayal

Sigmund Freud was already nineteen years old when Jung was born. The Freuds, who were Jewish, lived in Vienna, where being Jewish was most definitely not an advantage.

Sigmund's mother was a beauty. She was his father's third wife and about twenty years younger than Papa Freud. To complicate matters further, she was only two years older than Sigmund's half-brother Phillip.

Siggy loved his mommy. He **really** loved his mommy. He loved her so much that he wanted — albeit unconsciously — to "possess" her...as his father had "possessed" her before him.

This made young Sigmund very nervous. It bothered him so much that he rolled it around his brilliant mind until he had developed an entire theory of human psycho-sexual growth and development based on it (psychiatrists call that sort of thing "compensation").

In the process, Freud introduced the concept of the unconscious mind to the Western European world.

Oedipus Rex, the young man who slays his father and possesses his mother, had returned to the scene as alive as he had been in the drama of classical Greece.

Mama

Pierre Janet

"Zo leaving zo zoon?"

Jung went to study briefly with the famous Parisian psychiatrist.

Pierre Janet, a disciple of Charcot, whose investigations into dissociative states and multiple personalities fascinated Jung.

Jung eventually landed a good job at the Burgholzi (mental) hospital, working under the direction of Dr. Eugen Blueler, who was recognized as one of Europe's top Physicians of the Mind.

Professor Blueler

THAT'S ALL NICE FOR HIM BUT WHAT ABOUT ME?

I founded the whole damn psychoanalytic movement. It was built on **my** ideas, it used **my** methods, it was **my** creation. So why are these two "gentlemen" even in the picture? Simple: because I was Jewish. (So, by some retarded Goyim version of logic, **psychoanalysis** was Jewish!) The crap we Jews had to put up with in Vienna in the 1850s when I was getting started was not exactly a pleasure. Nothing was going to change so much for the better in my life time and I knew it. Frankly, I cared more about psychoanalysis than about myself. So, if we were to move this beautiful invention of mine out of the Jewish ghetto and into the safety and prosperity of the culture in power, then what the psychoanalytic movement needed was a few outstanding Christians. Especially eminent German Christians like Herr Bleuler! Both of us needed Bleuler.

Jung because he was Swiss. . .

...AND ME BECAUSE I WAS JEWISH.

The fact that Freud, like Jung, was interested in the Burgholzi Hospital was no coincidence. Its prestigious Professor Bleuler had adapted Freud's analytic perspective in working with hysterics and schizophrenics. This gave Freud the much-needed opportunity to move his theories out of Vienna and to distance psychoanalysis from what detractors referred to as "Jewish mystical psychiatry." In Freud's Vienna, Jews had only in his father's generation been granted the right to own property, to become citizens, and to begin to assume a visible face In the politics of the city.

I MEAN LIKE I DID FOUND THE WHOLE PSYCHOANALYTIC THING THERE, DOC.

BUT WHICH OF US IS A TRUE NATIVE SON OF OUR FATHERLAND, HERR PROFESSOR?

Jung prospered under Bleuler's mentorship. Bleuler was a hard-nosed scientist. He wouldn't settle for theories and speculation, he wanted solid, verifiable *proof*. In contrast to his earlier publication on occult phenomena, Jung's work under Bleuler centered on measuring physical reactions to changes in word **association**.

ASSOCIATION [also Free Association or Word Association]
A spontaneous flow of interconnected thoughts and images around a specific word or idea, determined by unconscious connections. Jung's work at Burgholzli Hospital on word association used by Freud as "free association."

Out of this experimental data a complex pattern of interrelationships of associations began to emerge. Jung would later identify this pattern as a **complex.**

COMPLEX
An emotionally charged group of ideas and/or images; at the center of which is an archetype or archetypal image. (We'll define archetype later.)

I am by nature and disposition a scientist. I have always placed great emphasis on grounding my highly intuitive theories in the world of the scientific. Here I am pictured with the galvanic machine that I used in my experiments at Burgholzi Hospital. In the end my experiments supported some of my earlier ideas.

In 1906 Jung publicly announced his support of Freud's controversial psychoanalysis. In 1907, the two finally met in Vienna. It was a very festive occasion, which delighted Doctor Siggy, who had looked forward to meeting his brilliant young disciple. The Freuds did most of the entertaining, and Jung did most of the talking.

Freud was impressed by Jung. Very impressed. Jung seemed to understand psychoanalysis on a level so profound that he and Freud spoke from soul to soul.

NOT ONLY WERE THEY SOUL BROTHERS PROFESSIONALLY, BUT FREUD AND JUNG HAD A THING OR TWO IN COMMON IN OTHER WAYS...

Freud was a good husband and an attentive father. Jung was pretty much the same. Freud, like his young chosen successor, lived his home life in accordance with the traditional values handed down to him through his family.

Freud and Jung wrote a whole bunch of letters to each other. That is where much of what we know about their relationship comes from.

But they didn't tell each other everything.

Although both men were fairly loving husbands, they shared the same view of what Freud referred to as "the brutal state of marriage."

Both men were attracted to women other than their wives.

Women found Freud attractive.

Women (sometimes the same women) found Jung attractive.

Both men had their share of dalliances (and troubles) with women other than their wives.

And both men looovvvvved to write letters.

Dear Professor Freud...

What Jung did NOT know...

...was that his wife Emma also wrote letters to Sigmund. Emma would write to Dr. Freud—her husband's teacher, mentor, friend, and professional benefactor—and confess that Carl's open relationship with his mistress and former patient Tony Wolf really bothered her. Although Freud occasionally offered some real advice, he generally recommended that Emma continue to stand by her talented but philandering young husband during these troubling times.

Emma, as many of us might do in her place, decided that there must be something wrong with **her** self if her husband felt the need to supplement her affection with that of another woman. So Carl, her ever-so-understanding husband, not only agreed with her, he suggested that she should enter analysis...with **him!** Which, amazingly enough, she did.

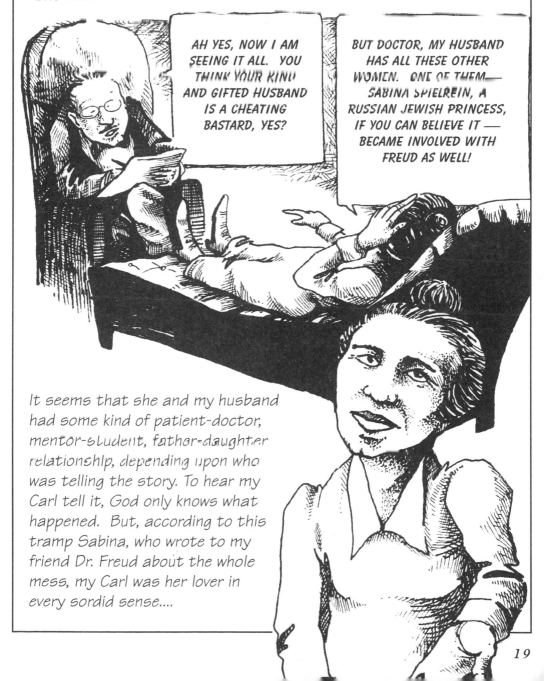

AH YES, NOW I AM SEEING IT ALL. YOU THINK YOUR KIND AND GIFTED HUSBAND IS A CHEATING BASTARD, YES?

BUT DOCTOR, MY HUSBAND HAS ALL THESE OTHER WOMEN. ONE OF THEM— SABINA SPIELREIN, A RUSSIAN JEWISH PRINCESS, IF YOU CAN BELIEVE IT — BECAME INVOLVED WITH FREUD AS WELL!

It seems that she and my husband had some kind of patient-doctor, mentor-student, father-daughter relationship, depending upon who was telling the story. To hear my Carl tell it, God only knows what happened. But, according to this tramp Sabina, who wrote to my friend Dr. Freud about the whole mess, my Carl was her lover in every sordid sense....

Jung, at one point, insisted to Sabina's mother that the whole matter was just so much fantasy and neurotic rubbish. At another time—in what was obviously a more combative mood—Dr. Jung not only pleaded his innocence, but demanded money for his professional services! The logic of it, Jung insisted to Freud, was impeccable. Whatever private thoughts Freud may have had about the matter, in public he defended his young friend and successor.

TALK ABOUT A SNOW JOB!! TO THIS MRS. SPIELREIN I WROTE SOMETHING ABOUT THE POWER OF THE TRANSFERENCE AND HOW THESE THINGS MUST BE TREATED WITH CAREFUL MEDICAL AND PSYCHIATRIC CONCERN. I ALSO, SINCE I TOO KNEW THIS SABINA, SAID SHE HAD A DARLING DAUGHTER. I ASSURED HER THAT DR. JUNG ENJOYED MY PERSONAL SUPPORT.

Sabina Spielrein, the Russian Jewish princess:

A MOST CONFUSING ASPECT OF HAVING AN AFFAIR OF THE HEART WITH CARL OR SIGGY, IS THAT ONE IS NEVER MERELY ONESELF. I AM SABINA...AND THE MISTRESS...AND THE ANIMA...AND THE TRAMP...AND...

The problem that, despite their much advertised sensitivity and intelligence, neither of these man-children could see, was **love**! I loved them—**both** of them. I was Dr. Jung's patient for awhile, then I became his lover. What I, a fine young Jewish princess from Russia, thought would be a perfect solution to the whole archetypal Jewish/Aryan problem, was for me to have Carl's child. This would enable me to selflessly unite Freudian and Jungian theories.

I told Siggy about my plans. He said I should get those crazy out of my head and marry a nice Jewish boy (which, just to spite him, I did). You should have seen the look on his face when I told him that I had decided to become a psychoanalyst!

Back in those early days when I was first getting started, psychoanalysts all tended to be a bit paranoid—and for good reason. It was not all that long ago that everyone associated with madness in any of its forms was thought to be tainted. And those of us who were fool enough to think we could cure it were considered the craziest of the lot. Everybody in the psychoanalytic movement had some kind of complex neurosis. We were all mad in one way or another! Most of the other docs we worked with thought we were either mad or practicing some medieval witchcraft.

Given my past and my continuing interest in parapsychology, Freud, ever the father, thought that the less I said about all that, the better. Especially, he confided, since he had decided to make me **his successor as the head of the psychoanalytic movement...**

Freud's appointment of Jung—who was young, Swiss, and Christian—as the new head of the psychoanalytic movement, did not go over very well in the land of the Viennese Shrinks. Freud's colleagues felt betrayed by his action, so they called a private meeting to discuss their displeasure. Freud, who had a nose for betrayal, burst in upon the meeting as if he'd been invited. He looked around the room. Finally he spoke:

"LOOK AT YOU. YOU ARE JEWISH. ALL OF YOU. ALL IS ABOUT TO BE LOST AND THE SWISS WILL SAVE US. NONE OF YOU KNOW WHAT IS TO COME. JUNG WILL KEEP US SAFE AND SECURE THE WORLD FOR OUR CHILDREN."

Freud was in tears. He didn't know how right he was. Or how wrong.

22

One of Jung's first tests as the head of the psychoanalytic movement involved a brilliant young analyst named Alfred Adler. Adler couldn't go along with Freud's notion that the psychosexual libido was the All-Powerful Force that Freud said it was. In Adler's view, man's most basic force was the drive for **power**. Rather than disagreeing with Adler's ideas as ideas, Adler was dismissed by Freud and his colleagues as simply neurotic; his ideas were relegated to the background.

Adler didn't do his credibility any good when he publicly denounced his Judaism and converted to Christianity. But to Jung, Adler was neither more nor less mad than the other shrinks. The dilemma that faced Jung in his new position of responsibility in the psychoanalytic movement was that now he must serve not only as the representative of the psychoanalytic party line, but as a peacemaker as well.

Jung thought long and hard about the difficulty between the two men. He ultimately decided that the problems that existed between Freud and Adler could best be explained by his developing theory of personal psychological type.

23

According to Jung's new theory, some people seemed to be born with an orientation toward *outward* validation; they sought comfort primarily from "external objects." Those people would be inclined to express their dual natures as EXTROVERTS.

INTROVERTS, conversely, would be people with an *inward* orientation.

"THERE YOU HAVE IT. THE PROBLEMS THAT WE ARE HAVING HERE WITH THESE TWO IS SIMPLY THAT ONE OF THEM, HERR FREUD, IS AN INTROVERT WHILE PROFESSOR ADLER IS AN EXTROVERT. NO WONDER THAT THEY DO NOT UNDERSTAND EACH OTHER: NOW THAT THE ANSWER IS CLEAR LET US PROCEED."

EXTROVERT

INTROVERT

THE ANSWER LIES WITHIN...

BY LOOKING OUTSIDE WE CAN UNDERSTAND THE DESIRE FOR POWER.

Needless to say, the matter did not end that simply. Adler was banished by Freud and his associates and had little choice but to go his own way. On top of that, the relationship between Freud and Jung was growing increasingly strained. Freud was not at all pleased when he learned of CG's heretical pronouncements in America that the Libido might have a much broader source than the narrowly sexual origin that Freud claimed it was. Jung had asserted that the Libido was one with the creative force of being. To Jung, the Libido was a life-force so large and all inclusive that Freud's "Id" and "Superego" were merely parts of it. The Libido, as Jung had come to see it, was both an expression of the instinctual primeval force to live and the tendency of the Higher Self to have life in consciousness.

Freud, the founder of the entire psychoanalytic tradition, the "inventor" of the unconscious mind, the doctor of "dreamology," was not amused. There was (to say the least) a strain in their relationship.

The strain became a split, professionally, with the publication of Freud's *Totem and Taboo* (1913). In *Totem*, Freud had ventured into "psychoanthropology," a branch of psychoanalysis that Jung considered his own exclusive turf. Not only did Jung take it as an affront, Freud had meant it as one: "Jung is crazy," Freud told his biographer Ernest Jones, "but I don't really want a split; I should prefer him to leave on his own accord. Perhaps my *Totem* work will hasten the break against my will." (Could a man as self-aware as Freud have deluded himself into thinking that he was hastening the break "against my will" when it was clearly his intention to do so? Who knows?)

In any case, both men had offended the other's pride and sense of territoriality.

THERE IS MORE TO THE LIBIDO THAN PRIMITIVE SEXUALITY! THE LIBIDO IS A LIFE FORCE, SO LARGE AND ALL-INCLUSIVE...

YOU HAVE STRAYED FROM THE ONE TRUE PATH OF PSYCHOANALYSIS!

The *professional* break between the two men was sad and regrettable. But their *personal* break was nearly ridiculous...

The end finally came as a result of a tragic misunderstanding.

It seemed that Binswanger, a mutual acquaintance and psychoanalytic colleague of both Freud and Jung, had fallen ill with some sort of tumor. Binswanger asked Freud to come and see him "under the cloak of the deepest secrecy." Binswanger didn't want the word of his illness spread into the professional community just at a time when his work was gaining some recognition. So Freud, fully aware that Jung lived not far from Binswanger — but sworn to secrecy — didn't mention the visit to Jung. When Jung got wind of the visit, he was offended and hurt. (These were passionate men — passionate in love, work, and friendship.) Jung was also suspicious that some intrigue might be playing out behind his back.

THAT DIRTY SNEAK — TRYING TO PULL A FAST ONE.

I MUST PROTECT BINSWANGER'S GOOD NAME.

Freud and Jung—to say the least—were exceptional men. Both men were strong-minded individuals who didn't shy away from facing the truth about themselves...and about us. Freud, by the weight of biological evidence, had scientifically affirmed the primacy of human bisexuality. Both men spoke of a time when bisexual or homosexual love among humans would be considered normal. Each man had acknowledged the sexual component of friendship in-general, and of theirs in particular.

It is a shame that things had to turn out so badly for these two great men who might have died the best of friends...or perhaps even "longtime companions."

Instead, two astonishingly open minds slammed shut like lids on coffins...

January 13, 1913

DR. JUNG,
YOUR LETTER CANNOT BE ANSWERED ...
I PROPOSE THAT WE ABANDON OUR
PERSONAL RELATIONS ENTIRELY....
I SHALL LOSE NOTHING BY IT....

Dr. Freud:

I ACCEDE TO YOUR WISH THAT WE
ABANDON PERSONAL RELATIONS, FOR
I NEVER THRUST MY FRIENDSHIP ON
ANYONE....
THE REST IS SILENCE...."

The rest
is silence.

Jung's Dark Night of the Soul

The events that followed immediately upon their separation in 1913 were of epic proportions for both men. But it was the younger Carl, now 38 years old who suffered most visibly. Freud had long since accepted the steady progression that had led toward their separation, but Jung was less prepared. He had a complete breakdown.

Jung called it the Nikia — "the night journey of the soul."

I WOULD NOW ENTER A PERIOD OF PROFOUND MADNESS.

Everything fell apart for Jung. He entered a period of regression verging on disintegration. His practice dwindled down to almost no one. He left his post as professor at the Zurich University. He resigned as chairman of the International Psychoanalytic Association. He had earlier parted ways with Bleuler, in the same way. He was isolated, alone, depressed, inconsolable. Only his devoted mistress Tony Wolf could quiet his soul as he sailed into the dark seas of his stormy inner life.

Having left both his practice and his teaching post, Jung returned for brief stays at the family home with Emma and his five children. But for the most part he preferred solitude on Lake Bollingen, which would remain an integral part of his long life. There he would walk down to the shore and build sand cities as he might have done as a child. He drew and he painted. He gave graphic form to the archetypal images of his deeper psychic life.

There are historical parallels in a group of myths depicting the physician as a wounded healer. Jung himself suggested, calling upon the Christ metaphor, that psychotherapists must learn to heal others through their own wounds.

So it should not be surprising to learn that the essential features of Jung's work originated in his own "wounds"—his own personality disorders. Especially his capacity for dissociation. This tendency to "split off" various aspects of his personality into separate compartments can be traced throughout Jung's life and work. While it might be too much to suggest that Jung had a Multiple Personality Disorder, he certainly would fall well within the continuum of Dissociative Identity Disorders.

Jung would spend much of his life resolving a critical split between his own personalities....

Jung was aware of at least two separate and distinct aspects of his own psychology. These he referred to as his No. 1 and No. 2 personalities. Number 1 was more defined by the interior world of maternal engulfment than it was by separation and **individuation**.

Number 1 personality

I HAVE TRULY COSMIC CONSCIOUSNESS.

INDIVIDUATION
The conscious realization of one's unique psychological reality, including both strengths and limitations. C.G.JUNG: "I use the term 'individuation' to denote the process by which a person becomes a psychological 'in-dividual,' that is, a separate, indivisible unity or 'whole.'"

Number 2 personality

DAD

I'M JUST A SIMPLE SWISS FARMER.

Number 2 personality was ruled more by Jung's rational aspect. The aspect that he might have said was "governed by the Logos (the word) or the father." It was this side that was most readily **constellated** into the wise and loving father.

CONSTELLATE or **CONSTELLATED**
Whenever there is a strong emotional and/or psychic reaction to a person, situation, or psychosocial environment, a 'complex' has been 'constellated.' (activated or triggered)

From 1913 at age 38 to 1919, Jung embarked upon a "self-experiment" at the moment of his greatest uncertainty, trying to understand the fantasies and other elements that surfaced from his unconscious... and trying also to come to terms with them. During this "night journey" Jung would experience psychological and spiritual upheavals of mythic proportions.

He would meet Philemon [a friend and convert of St. Paul].

This involved the employment of ancient yoga and meditation techniques. Often this would be accompanied by feelings of great emotion. Contrary to his expectations, it turned out that his fantasies and images had no reference point in his own personal experience. Jung recalls that the "contents were archetypal, originating in an impersonal psychic realm, the Collective Unconscious." In one epochal dream, the unconscious contents of the Western and Northern European mind pressed into consciousness to reveal themselves in the symbols that would foreshadow the coming of the Second World War. *CGJ*

"I was seized by an overpowering vision. I saw a monstrous flood covering all of the northern and low lying lands between the North Sea and the Alps.

The mountains of Switzerland grew higher....I realized a great catastrophe was in progress....I saw the rubble of civilization...the drowned bodies of thousands... then the whole sea turned to blood...."

"So I went down to the lake to build sand castles and to the yard outside my office to build miniature villages. The small boy is still around and possesses a creative life that I lack." **CGJ**

Gnostic   Bible

Jung turned both in desperation and new-found hope to the Gnostic Bible and the early texts of medieval **alchemy**. All the world was open to exploration. He thirsted after the symbolic and the mythical throughout human history.

ALCHEMY

The older form of chemistry, which combined experimental chemistry with general, symbolic, intuitive, semi-religious speculations about nature and man. The alchemist was said to pursue the secret method of turning material into gold. The alchemist also was ultimately seeking the "secret of God" in the unknown substance.

My dear colleagues. Yes, for this purpose that's who you are. You are my colleagues. We are all students, put here by God to learn. You do know and understand that I do mean God? The Living God. This for me has always been obvious. My father believed in God too...but the way I see it, my father didn't think God liked him. He shouldn't have taken it so personally.

After all, there was a time when God didn't seem to like anybody...

VOCATUS ATQUE NON VOCATUS ADERIT

THAT INSCRIPTION ABOVE THE DOOR OF OUR HOME IN SWITZERLAND?—I'LL TRANSLATE IT FOR YOU: "SUMMONED OR NOT GOD WILL BE THERE."

Freud, Jung and the Holocaust

The story of Freud and Jung did not end with their separation in 1913. Each continued to influence and inform the other's work. This was no less true among the followers of Freudian Psychoanalysis and Jungian Analytic Psychology. Members of both schools would push against the assumptions of the other in an effort to find meaning and healing in each perspective. But, cast against the atrocities of World War II, lingering shadows would remain concerning "the Jewish Question."

In the end, was it simply their cultural and political differences that divided them? Or was it worse? Was it the "Jewish thing?" Before the story was over, Jung would stand accused of having allowed, if not endorsed the publication under his editorship of a statement of policy that Psychoanalysis would be practiced in a manner consistent with the proclamations of Adolf Hitler and the German Third Reich.

Nowadays, Psychoanalysis is considered either science or not. In Freud's day, according to Professor Jerry Diller, Ph.D., writing in *Freud's Jewish Identity*, it was an altogether different story:

The history of psychoanalysis is inextricably bound up with its founder Sigmund Freud. To most people in turn-of-the-century Vienna, psychoanalysis was virtually indistinguishable from its Jewish origins. Freud was, of course, Jewish. And he first presented his radical theories not before some august medical group, but in lectures to the B'nai B'rith, a Jewish fraternal order.

The foundations of analytic psychology are at least equally a product of Jung's decidedly Christian origins. If Freud's psychoanalysis is of Moses the monotheistic patriarch, then clearly Jung's analytic psychology is that of Jesus the Son. At least to the same extent, it should be recalled that both men were Germans, albeit two separate and distinct hybrid Swiss and Jewish mutations of an essentially Germanic consciousness. (Diller — *Freud's Jewish Identity*)

In his youth Freud had in fact identified strongly with Germany and with German culture. As a student, for instance, he belonged to the 'Leserverein der Deutschen Studenten,' a student fraternity that advocated the annexation of Austria by Germany proper. His fascination with all things German faded quickly, however, when he realized the intimate connection between German nationalism and anti-Semitism.

During most of his adult life, however, Freud's view reflected the words of this mentor Joseph Breur who described himself as a "Jew by origin and a German by nature."

"MY LANGUAGE IS GERMAN. MY CULTURE, MY ATTAINMENTS ARE GERMAN. I CONSIDERED MYSELF GERMAN INTELLECTUALLY, UNTIL I NOTICED THE GROWTH OF ANTI-SEMITIC PREJUDICE IN GERMANY AND GERMAN AUSTRIA."
FREUD

With the rise of National Socialism and its institutionalization of anti-Semitism, the campaign against Freud and the psychoanalysts grew. His books and those of his followers were publicly burned in Berlin for their "soul-destroying overemphasis on the sex drive."

One cannot help but to be struck by the manner in which Freud, who wouldn't be intimidated even by Hitler, retorted in the face of Nazi insults.

In a letter to Wilhelm Reich, he remarks about Hitler:

"MANY PEOPLE HERE WON-
DERED HOW IN A MIDSUMMER
NIGHT'S DREAM SHAKESPEARE
COULD MAKE A LADY FALL IN
LOVE WITH A DONKEY. AND
NOW JUST THINK OF IT, A
NATION OF SIXTY-FIVE MILLION
HAS DONE THE SAME THING."
FREUD

"WHAT PROGRESS WE ARE MAK-
ING. IN THE MIDDLE AGES THEY
WOULD HAVE BURNED ME. NOW
THEY ARE CONTENT WITH BURN-
ING MY BOOKS.
WELL AT LEAST I CAN TAKE SOME
PRIDE IN THE FACT THAT I TOO
AM BEING BURNED IN THE BEST
OF COMPANY." **FREUD**

As Nazism spread, Jewish analysts were systematically harassed, driven out of scientific and psychological associations, replaced by their Aryan counterparts and eventually forced to flee for their lives. By 1938, the year Freud was finally given permission by the Nazis to leave Vienna for London, the Nazi plan for liquidating the "Jewish science" in Germany was virtually complete.

Freud and Jung were both more interested in the politics of the inner life than in the politics between countries. Perhaps this in part accounts for each man's naiveté in the face of National Socialism. Freud often placed the welfare of psychoanalysis before his Jewishness. Although there is some evidence that Freud suspected Jung of a disguised anti-Semitism, he would not allow himself to be aware of it. When he and his Jewish colleagues were forced to bring the question to consciousness, Freud defended Jung.

After all, Freud himself had selected Jung as his heir apparent.

What if the crown prince moved the headquarters of psychoanalysis to Zurich?.

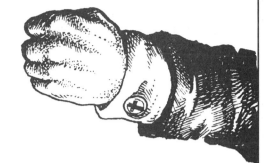

By the time the fourth International Psychoanalytic Congress was held, the battle lines had been drawn between the Christian Swiss and the Jewish Viennese. Racial tensions were out in the open and being addressed by Freud, Maeder, Ferenzi, Karl Abraham, and others.

Abraham suggested that, since many of the members were no longer comfortable with Jung's leadership, a vote of confidence was called for. Those opposed to Jung abstained. A third of the members followed this course.

The year was 1913. Jung and Freud would never see each other again after that meeting. Karl Abraham was appointed temporary president. Then, as if to put an exclamation point behind the racial roots of the conflict, Ernest Jones, himself a non-Jew, would report that at the conclusion of the Congress Jung turned to him and said in an accusing tone,

I THOUGHT YOU WERE A CHRISTIAN!

In *Lingering Shadows*, a C.G. Jung Foundation book, Andrew Samuels asks, "Is there something in the fundamental structure of Jung's thinking about the Jews, in its heart or essences, that makes it inevitable that he could develop the degree of anti-Semitism that would concern us?... When Jung writes about the Jews and Jewish psychology, is there something in his whole attitude that brings him into the same frame as the Nazis?...Is there something to Worry about?... My brief answer is yes!"

By 1937 German anti-Semiticism was rampant and plans for the systematic annihilation of the Jews were well under way. It was then, at the mature age of 60 that Jung felt called upon to attempt, "an Aryan psychology"... One better suited to the Germans than the Jewish psychology of Sigmund Freud.

Adolf Guggenbuhl-Craig, a Jew and a renowned Jungian analyst says, "Jung certainly was anti-Semitic. But everyone in Europe was anti-Semitic. The Jews were considered to be Christ killers. Europe was dominated by appeasers."

But as for Jung, was he a mere appeaser? During the reign of Hitler's Third Reich, Jung would serve until 1939 as the editor of the German language "Zen Trablett fur Psychotherapie." In it there were repeated attacks on "Jewish mental states" and a great lauding of Northern Aryan psychology. There was also much praise for Hitler and the Nazi party. Jung even gave some measure of support to the idea of exterminating mental patients.

I GUESS I SLIPPED UP. CGJ

In the world of art as in the world of race, Hitler believed in final solutions. Both eminent and amateur Nazi psychiatrists and sympathizers joined in the fray condemning cubism, constructivism, expressionism and surrealism. All of this and more was simply the work of degenerate madmen whose works were hatched in the asylum cage.

It was in 1932, during a low point in his ascension toward much longed for fame, that Jung offers the following discussion of the work of Pablo Picasso... Having first described Picasso as a case of latent schizophrenia, he goes on... "An artist fatefully drawn into the dark, who follows not the accepted ideals of goodness and beauty, but the demonical attraction of ugliness and evil. It is these anti-Christian and Luciferian forces that well up in modern man."

CG Jung
Picasso....
Degenerate

"Picasso and his exhibition are a sign of the times, just as much as the twenty-eight thousand people who came to look at his picture." **CGJ**

Although Switzerland lay virtually under siege surrounded by the Third Reich, Jung in Zurich gave sanctuary to Jewish analysts and their families as Freud had earlier predicted he might. By 1942, at no small risk to his own personal safety, Jung was openly referring to Hitler as the Anti-Christ. Then, in 1943, he made public his support of the Allied Forces.

Jung's little book Wotan is perhaps the most frightening mythological description available on National Socialism. All other explanations, based on economy, inflation, sociology and, the like pale by comparison to this powerful mythic imagery.

NEVER AGAIN

"Now Germany must suffer the consequences of its pact with the Devil". But ever the optimist, Jung adds, "where sin is great, there also grace might more abound."

(1946) CGJ

42

THE FATE OF SABINA SPIELREIN

Jung's lover of an earlier time, Sabina Spielrein, would become a psychoanalyst and remain associated with Sigmund Freud. Even so, she could never fully give up her attachment to Carl Jung. She returned to Russia to practice psychoanalysis until it was banned by Joseph Stalin.

Sabina lived in Rostov, Russia until the Nazis invaded the Soviet Union. During the early stages of the Occupation, all the Jews in the city, including Sabina and her daughters, were taken to the synagogue and shot.

THE DEATH OF SIGMUND FREUD

Freud, unlike his extended Eastern European family, was not murdered by the Germans.

He made his passage to England safely, but not before his daughter Anna was detained by Gestapo and additional money was extorted from the Freuds.

A year after his move to England, Freud had a recurrence of cancer of the mouth and jaw.

On August 1, 1939 Freud closed his practice. He died at home the following month. He was 83.

July 25, 1942

September 23, 1939

JUNG:

The Work

Most books on Jung deal with his Nazi period by either ignoring it, minimizing it, or tucking it away neatly in an Appendix. The author of this book finds Jung's Nazism too hideous to ignore, too enormous to minimize, and too reprehensible to bury in an Appendix. So I have begun this book by showing Jung at his worst.

Now, with that behind us (or hovering over us), let us take a look at the work that has made Jung one of the two pillars of modern psychiatry. Jung almost singlehandedly gave scientific respectability to Religion and Myth, to Intuition and Spirituality, to God and *the gods*. Freud, for all his brilliance, shrunk us until we were nothing but genitals with high I.Q.s. Jung, for all his flaws, gave us back our Souls.

The Foundations of Jungian Psychology

The original followers of the Freudian Psychoanalytic movement tended to view the patient as a closed system. It was the analyst's job to observe the patient and to record behavior. They operated under the assumption that the analyst's own psychology was of little or no importance in influencing the patient or interpreting his words. This was an application, whole cloth, of the medical, surgical, scientific method as they had come to understand it. Jung's initial approach to the study of the human behavior was very much influenced by the practice of psychiatry in his approach to experimental research. It was in this same spirit that he learned Freud's methods.

Jung paid tribute throughout his long life to the importance of psychoanalysis in the scientific and therapeutic fields. He understood the nature of the psychodynamic method. He fully grasped the importance of transference in which the patient's perceptions of the therapist are distorted by the patient's external and internal experience most of which was motivated by powerful unconscious forces no longer available to conscious awareness.

But in spite of the similarities in their initial approach, Jung came to differ radically from Freud. The conflicts that separated them were serious and fundamental, especially regarding the relative importance of infantile sexuality and the psychology of religion. At the fourth International Psychoanalytic Congress in Munich, Jung had designated his own psychology as Analytic Psychology. One year later, Jung and his Zurich colleagues resigned from the International Psychoanalytic Association.

I KNEW THAT FREUD WOULD EVENTUALLY GET SO INFURIATED BY MY INDEPENDENCE THAT OUR FRIENDSHIP WOULD COME TO AN END. I DIDN'T REALLY WANT THAT BUT I JUST COULD NOT GO ALONG WITH THE IDEA THAT INFANTILE AND REPRESSED SEXUALITY EXPLAINED EVERYTHING. IT JUST DOESN'T.

MY SCHIZOPHRENIC PATIENTS AT BURGHOLZI MENTAL HOSPITAL, FOR EXAMPLE, HAD A LOT MORE WRONG WITH THEM THAN A SIMPLE CASE OF UNRESOLVED CONFLICT.

THERE HAS TO BE MORE TO IT. I'M INCLINED TO GO ALONG WITH THE NEUROLOGICAL AND ORGANIC EXPLANATIONS.

In most cases of psychosis the patient loses all sense of reality. The illness is so extreme that it has to involve the loss of other instinctual functions as well as the sex drive. But Freud would have us all maintain that reality is a function of sex. Clearly, the Libido that drives the engine of what makes us who we are must be redefined!

Some fourteen years would pass until 1928 when Jung, age 53, would publish his definitive volume, *Two Essays on Analytic Psychology*. Here he described his controversial conclusions. He discussed at some length how two different interpretations might be made of the same material; the sexual interpretation identified with Psychoanalysis, and the ego interpretation identified with individual psychology. He considered psychoanalysis to be "Extroverted" and analytic psychology to be "Introverted." At the time, the distinctions between the various schools of analytic thought had not yet received the benefit of the "Ego Psychologists."

Jung came to believe that both the analytic method and the educative method were particularly relevant to those patients who were in the "first half of life." But there was more that could be done for the patient in whom Jung was most interested, those who had entered the "second half of life."

Young people may indeed suffer from the consequence of infantile sexual trauma. We often see this in cases of hysteria and obsessional neurosis. The analytic method may in such cases effect a cure. Other times the troubles of the young are more like problems of orientation. Here there is a need for the educative method.

But it has been my experience that for those patients over thirty-five who have entered the second half of life, the problem is usually spiritual in nature.
CGJ

The Structure of the Psyche

Jung's idea of the human psyche and its structure is grounded in Freudian psychology and in many respects parallels classic psychoanalytic thought. But Jung was not a systematic thinker and his writing does not present the neat linear pattern of his predecessor. The illustration that follows presents a holistic picture of the human soul as Jung came to understand it:

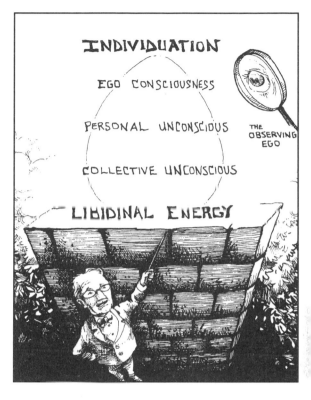

INDIVIDUATION

EGO CONSCIOUSNESS

PERSONAL UNCONSCIOUS

COLLECTIVE UNCONSCIOUS

LIBIDINAL ENERGY

THE OBSERVING EGO

WE MUST COME TO KNOW THE ESSENTIAL NATURE OF OUR SOULS.

EGO
PERSONAL
COLLECTIVE
LIBIDINAL ENERGY

This illustration should be envisioned as a kind of three-dimensional cone rather than a flat pyramid. The very top represents the "conscious ego" or the immediate knower of what is going on as we come to understand it through the senses. This is a relatively small part of the experience of being and includes all of those aspects of reality that are available to immediate recall: memories, knowledge of facts, places, names, dates, etc.

The observing ego

This consciousness, while it is the "ego," needs to be differentiated from the "observing ego." The psyche not only includes the knowing ego but the ability to observe oneself in the very process of both knowing and being. It is as though the ego has established the fact that I am here while the observing ego knows that I am here knowing that I am here.

I HAVE TO ADMIT THAT I GOT SOME OF THESE IDEAS FROM MY EARLIER READING OF THE PHILOSOPHY OF EMMANUEL KANT.

The "personal unconscious" is for Jung just what it was for Freud. It is made up of those things that have grown out of one's own individual experience, but have been forgotten or repressed in service to and in defense of the ego. This is that part of the individual experience that one has suppressed. These are things that we don't want to know about, things that are no longer brought to memory but remain part of our own personal experience.

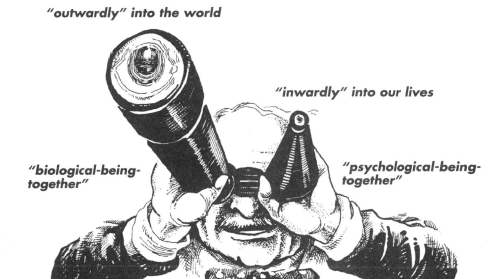

"outwardly" into the world

"inwardly" into our lives

"biological-being-together"

"psychological-being-together"

The collective unconscious represents the larger aspect of the individual psyche or soul. "The true history of the spirit is not preserved in learned volumes or in memory, but in the living organism of every individual."

As we look not only "inwardly" into our lives but also "outwardly" into the world, it becomes apparent that we all share not only a "biological-being-together," but also a "psychological-being-together."

We not only share those things about which we are "collectively aware," but we also share those things about which we are "collectively unaware."

What causes the behavior of the whole of humanity?

It is from this vision of the human psyche, according to Ira Progoff, that Jung developed what became a social psychology. Progoff states in *Jung and Social Meaning* that the major significance of Jung's idea of the collective unconscious is that it presents a framework for understanding not only what causes individuals to do what they do but what causes the behavior of the whole of humanity as well.

> The state of being toward which the psyche is tending I refer to as "individuation." This "individuation" can be understood in personal terms as a process whereby one becomes most wholly and most fully one's own unique self, which is different from everything and everyone else who has ever been. We move toward individuation both singularly and collectively.

THIS "INDIVIDUATION..."

There is a force...
that transcends our individual reality that seeks expression throughout the whole of existence.

There is a force that transcends our individual reality that seeks expression throughout the whole of existence. This was the "libidinal force" that Freud had developed as a concept to expand our understanding of instinct, heredity, and the sexual impulse. Jung came to refer to the "libido" as the life force of the historical universe which achieves its ultimate expression in the unified Self.

The Personality Types

One comes into life, according to Jung, constellating a direction and movement toward "introversion" or "extroversion." The extrovert moves out into the world. The introvert moves in an inward direction. These are not static states of being but change over the course of time and personal development. Jung saw the human personality in a way that very much paralleled current notions about the evolution of the universe: that it expands; that it contracts; that we progress; that we regress. This dynamic pattern of being establishes a polarity that attracts its opposite. If we are, for example, extroverted during the first half of our life, it is likely that we will be introverted during the second half.

EXTROVERSION

INTROVERSION

54

Jung established four principle functions of the personality within which the complexes of our individual psychologies find expression. The conception of "psychological types" was developed in the *Psychological Factors Determining Human Behavior* and includes "sensation," "thinking," "feeling," and "intuition."

Thinking and feeling he regarded as rational functions and sensation and intuition as non-rational. Any one of these functions might dominate the consciousness at any given developmental point. The individual will use the dominant function to orient the whole of one's psychic life.

THINKING	FEELING	SENSATION	INTUITION

If, for example, a person is dominated by thinking, the emphasis will be placed upon the rational functions of measurement, data analysis, and empirical knowing. Those dominated by feeling are caught up in the world of the affect. The sensate person will turn first toward what can be known by hearing, tasting, seeing, smelling and gathering through the senses. Intuition enables one to know from within without regard to reason. It is an immediate apprehension.

Jung looked upon the functions as an orientation to the understanding of the conscious and unconscious processes of the developing personality. He looked upon the process as a function compass in which the inferior function moves beyond compensation toward fuller equilibrium with the dominant function. (Progoff)

The first English translation of Jung's theories of psychological types was first made available in 1923. Later Joseph Wheelwright developed the Wheelwright Personality Inventory based upon Jung's typology.

Isabel Briggs-Myers

It was Kathryn Briggs who in the summer of 1942 undertook the development of the Myers-BriggsType Indicator with her daughter Isabel Briggs-Myers. Today this test instrument may be the most standardized and widely used application of Jung's typology.

"THE MERIT OF JUNG'S THEORY OF PERSONALITY TYPE IS THAT IT ENABLES US TO EXPECT SPECIFIC PERSONALITY DIFFERENCES IN PARTICULAR PEOPLE AND TO COPE WITH PEOPLE AND THEIR DIFFERENCES IN A CONSTRUCTIVE WAY."

"WHATEVER THE CIRCUMSTANCES OF YOUR LIFE, WHATEVER YOUR PERSONAL TIES, WORK, AND RESPONSIBILITIES, THE UNDERSTANDING OF TYPE CAN MAKE YOUR PERCEPTIONS CLEARER, YOUR JUDGMENTS SOUNDER AND YOUR LIFE CLOSER TO YOUR HEART'S DESIRE." (BRIGGS-MYERS)

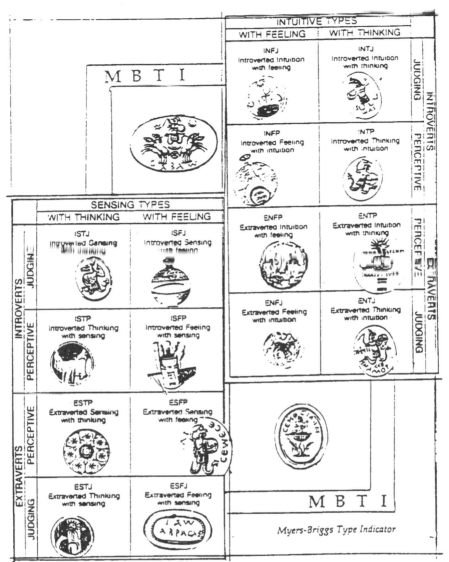

		INTUITIVE TYPES			
		WITH FEELING	WITH THINKING		
		INFJ Introverted Intuition with feeling	INTJ Introverted Intuition with thinking	JUDGING	INTROVERTS
		INFP Introverted Feeling with intuition	INTP Introverted Thinking with intuition	PERCEPTIVE	
		ENFP Extraverted Intuition with feeling	ENTP Extraverted Intuition with thinking	PERCEPTIVE	EXTRAVERTS
		ENFJ Extraverted Feeling with intuition	ENTJ Extraverted Thinking with intuition	JUDGING	

M B T I

		SENSING TYPES			
		WITH THINKING	WITH FEELING		
INTROVERTS	JUDGING	ISTJ Introverted Sensing with thinking	ISFJ Introverted Sensing with feeling		
	PERCEPTIVE	ISTP Introverted Thinking with sensing	ISFP Introverted Feeling with sensing		
EXTRAVERTS	PERCEPTIVE	ESTP Extraverted Sensing with thinking	ESFP Extraverted Sensing with feeling		
	JUDGING	ESTJ Extraverted Thinking with sensing	ESFJ Extraverted Feeling with sensing		

M B T I

Myers-Briggs Type Indicator

As Jung points out in *Psychological Types*, mankind is equipped with two distinct and sharply contrasting ways of perceiving. One means is "sensing" and the other is "intuition." He also said that we come to conclusions and make judgments through the employment of the thinking and feeling functions. These latter attributes he referred to as "rational functions" while sensation and intuition were considered "non-rational functions."

57

The Dynamic of the Archetype

The core of Jung's analytic psychology is made up of the "archaic remnants" of the psychic history of the human species. These remnants of human experience have come to form "primordial images" which are more than intellectual postulates. This is the "archetype" or "model from which all things of the same kind are made."

ARCHETYPE
Universal patterns or motifs which come from the collective unconscious and are the basic content of religions, mythologies, legends, and fairytales; emerging in individuals in the form of dreams, visions and fantasies. The archetype carries specific energy and is capable of acting upon the world. (You might want to read that last sentence twice.)

The archetype is a phenomena of "numinos" or "God-like" dimensions. The archetype is in a very real sense alive and functioning in the world. The archetypes thus have their own initiative and their own specific energy. These powers enable them both to produce a meaningful interpretation and to interfere in a given situation. CGJ

In this sense they are not unlike the character of the personal complex. But while the personal complex grows out of individual history, the archetypal complex is born of our collective history. The collective complex gives rise to mythical systems, ideals and values that are of a universal quality. They are thus formulated in response to the universal aspects of human experience. They exist to explain, to compensate, to understand, to give meaning to creation and life, to destruction and death.

The archetype of the anima and the animus

Jung distinguished a set of symbols, dream images, and projections as referring specifically to either the masculine or the feminine.

These he refers to using the Latin name for the female soul-image **anima** and the male soul-image **animus**.

ANIMA and ANIMUS

Personification of the feminine nature of a man's unconscious and the masculine nature of a woman's. Anima and animus manifest themselves most typically as figures in dreams and fantasies ("dream girl," "dream lover"), or in the irrationalities of a man's <u>feeling</u> and a woman's <u>thinking</u>. As regulators of behavior they are two of the most influential archetypes.

(This is the simple version; the concept will be expanded in later chapters.)

Feminine and masculine conscious psycho-social adaptations define our social mask or what Jung refers to as the persona. Women are supposed to act real lady-like and men are to act more manly-like.

But on the inside where these projections become unconscious introjections, we experience the opposite sex as the lost part of our own selves.

Jung held that the psyche contained within it the tendency to compensate in its attempt to achieve balance. There is, he believed, in each man a feminine side and in each female a masculine side. Later Jungians, as we shall see, came to define these terms more broadly.

Jung claimed that there is a biological basis for these sexual opposites within the personality. In each man there is a majority of male genes and a minority of female genes; and the opposite holds true for women. The anima corresponds to the female minority in men; and the animus to the male minority in women.

The archetypes are constellated around four basic patterns of human activity...

- the **static feminine**

- the **dynamic masculine**

- the **static masculine**

- the **dynamic feminine**

These patterns were initially based on the work of Erick Neumann, who identified the elementary and transformative aspects of the feminine principle.

The patterns were further developed by Gareth Hill, PhD, teacher and Jungian analyst. Hill's theoretical work, as it appears in *Masculine and Feminine*, transcends the patriarchal bias that influenced Jung and his followers. Hill presents us with a "contra sexual image" of psychic life that transcends gender linkage.

Static Feminine
Positive

The static feminine takes its elemental image from the containing uterus—moist, dark, surrounding and holding fast to what is gestating within it. This is the Great Mother. It is interdependent being and is undifferentiated. The positive social manifestation of this archetypal pattern can be recognized in the evolution of the homogeneity which makes group life possible.

Mother Complex

The Mother Complex is constellated within this quadrant.

Men who draw their psychic energy from within the Static Feminine might later come to suffer the inheritance of the **Puer Aeternus** [Latin for "eternal youth"] — the son who must remain forever young.

This is the Peter Pan Complex of modernity.

MaMa!

This is the Great Mother

Good Golly, Miss Kali!

Static Feminine
NEGATIVE

The negative aspect, when pervasive enough, can reach disastrous dimensions. It is indifferent to the fate of the individual as it ceaselessly creates, nurtures, destroys and devours. Change is abhorred.

This is the devouring Mother.

Dynamic Masculine
Positive

The dynamic masculine stands opposite to the static feminine and takes the image of the penetrating phallus. It is expressed in initiative and action directed toward a goal. It is expressed instinctually in mating and the strategies of the hunt. This is the Hero, the master, the conqueror in service to differentiated individualism.

Its positive social value is associated with cognitive development, linear expression, and the harnessing of nature in the service of humanistically-oriented technology.

this is the animus, the hero, the strategies of the hunt.

Dynamic Masculine
NEGATIVE

Its negative aspect takes form in its excesses. The creative thrust is perverted into destructiveness, violence. and disregard for the natural environment.

This is the hero gone mad.

Static Masculine
Positive

The static masculine stands opposite the dynamic feminine. It is the tendency toward organization of individuals into systems of order. In nature we see its expression in the herd. At the human level it is expressed in the patriarchal culture pattern and the establishment of hierarchical social organizations. It uses its systems and codes in the service of nonpersonal objectivity and its monuments include science, government, and the law. Its ultimate social value is the preservation of order and adaptation is valued more highly than authenticity in social interactions.

Father Complex

The Father Complex is constellated in this quadrant.
Its consequent outcome may take the form of the animus-bound woman.

Static Masculine
NEGATIVE

Its negative aspect is also found in its excess, which leads to order and organization for their own sake. The petty, dehumanizing righteousness and lifelessness of many bureaucracies present a vivid example.

Too much of the Great Father.

Dynamic Feminie
Positive

The dynamic feminine stands opposite the static masculine. Its tendency is toward undirected movement, toward the new, the nonra-
tional, the playful. It is the flow of
experience, yielding and responsive
to be acted upon. In nature it is
expressed as the random movement
underlying environmental evolution
and genetic mutation. At the human
level it finds expression in the creative process. It is the archetypal
maiden calling us to new unions, com-
binations, insights, and awareness.
Its effect is transformed awareness.
Its social expression is in participa-
tion and process.

ITS EFFECT IS TRANSFORMED AWARENESS.

This is the anima, the muse, the creative, the good angel.

NICE WORK IF YOU CAN GET IT...

This is just too much.

Dynamic Feminine
NEGATIVE

Its negative aspect lies
in its excess where
transformed awareness
and altered states of
consciousness lead away
from synthesis toward
disintegration and chaos.
The negative state
includes alcohol and drug
dependence, hysteria,
identity diffusion, and
certain psychoses.

Dr. Hill has developed his formulations of these four archetypal patterns to form a developmental psychology.
(Jung's work, on the other hand, stopped short of estab-
lishing a systematic theory of development.) Hill empha-
sizes the dynamism that is generated as a compensatory
movement away from each of the static poles, through the
dynamic pole, to the opposite static pole. He pictures
this dynamism as follows:

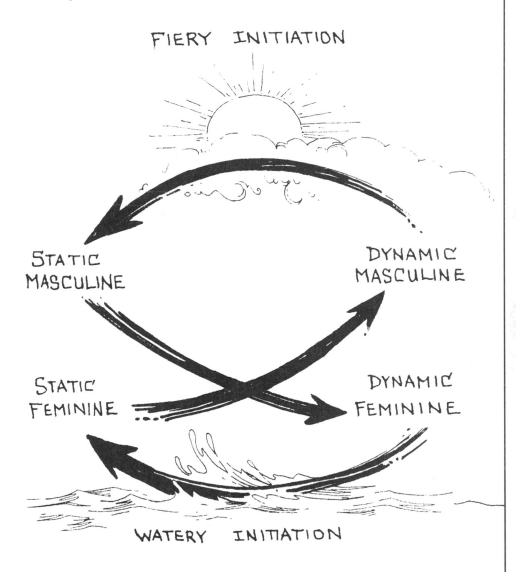

FIERY INITIATION

STATIC
MASCULINE

DYNAMIC
MASCULINE

STATIC
FEMININE

DYNAMIC
FEMININE

WATERY INITIATION

Jungian Analytic Psychology

This dynamism describes the development of the individual as understood by both Freud and Jung. In their formulation, we see the child moving away from the undifferentiated mother toward becoming a separate individual who achieves static maturity and a final spiritual level of self-expression. This is a movement through differentiation, individuation, and integration.

INDIVIDUATION

DIFFERENTIATION

INTEGRATION

Each epoch in the process of psychological development calls forth a period of initiation.

TRIAL BY FIRE

As the soul or psyche moves from the Dynamic Masculine pole of heroic initiation, one passes through "the trial by fire," in which we learn about submission to authority.

WATERY INITIATIONS

Then, moving from the idealized pole of the Static Masculine, we enter a "period of watery initiations," in which we are transformed through the auspices of the Dynamic Feminine.

Finally we return once again to the mirroring pole of the Static Feminine where we began in undifferentiated containment.

Jung discovered that by taking his own dreams and the dreams of his patients seriously, he could find the key to understanding the "secret background to life," which contained hidden solutions to people's everyday problems. He, like Freud before him, found in dreams "the royal road to **the unconscious**." The psyche contained a healer within itself which could be activated by exploring dreams and fantasies.

The UNconscious

It is important to note that The Unconscious is <u>not</u> just below the surface of consciousness (i.e. subconscious) but is quite literally unknown. (i.e. not available to consciousness). However unknown it may be, the unconscious strongly influences the individual. (In Jung's view, our common 'collective' unconscious influences the whole of the universe.)

For Jung, the meaningfulness of dreams is taken for granted. And the message of the dream is experienced as fact. (Segaller & Berger)

DREAMS according to C.G. JUNG:

"The dream is a little hidden door in the innermost and most secret recesses of the soul.... It is from the all-uniting depths that the dream arises, be it ever so childish, grotesque, and immoral.... Dreams...are natural phenomena which are nothing other than what they pretend to be. They do not deceive, they do not lie, they do not distort or disguise, but naively announce what they are and what they mean."

The most important theme in the Jungian approach to dreams is that the dream itself is a natural human activity. Jung's view that the unconscious is active and independent automatically suggests that any expression of the unconscious is worth considering in its own right. Dreams, since they were expressions of the unconscious, could provide a compensatory perspective in one's conscious life.

The nature of the material in dreams prompted Jung repeatedly to ask the same question. Were the images and complexes in the unconscious purely the result of repressed, uncomfortable feelings from conscious life, as Freud had suggested, or did they have an independent existence, as if inherited from human evolution, rather than the chronological lifetime of the individual? Jung, in the final analysis, was quite satisfied that much of the content of individual dreams arises out of our collective or archetypal experience. He saw the archetypal complex repeated in dreams, fantasies, stories, myths, and the recollections of our common human history.

The archetypal figures of our individual and collective dream lives include: the Ego, the Shadow, the Persona, the Anima/Animus, the Self, the Mother, the Father, the Puer/Divine Child, the Kore/Maiden, the Hero, the Wise Old Man, the Trickster, the Androgyne and the Coniunctio.

Whether dreams replay the horrors of war, direct us to a lost pencil, comment upon our attitude to the natural world, or review the sum of our individual life, there was no doubt in Jung's mind that the dream had wisdom. For Carl Jung and his followers, the dream is an experience to be lived, to be listened to, and to be applied to the way we live and regard our individual and collective lives. (Segaller & Berger)

...Jung's mind was peopled by many characters; should his book be any different..?

Welcome to Eranos

I'm Frau Olga Frobe Kapteyn. You can call me Olga. Any friend of Herr Doctor is a friend of mine. Let me welcome you to Eranos. I started up this little retreat on the shores of Lake Maggiore in Northern Italy not far from the Swiss border. It was my hope that the best minds of our time might gather here together and share their wisdom.

Professor Jung was a perfect addition. His popular confabs were just fabulous. Why, we had visitors from all over the world and some big names too. I could go on and on but let's just quietly go on in and listen to the Professor...

There is no general theory of dreams. Although all dreams clearly do have a message, the meaning of the dream symbol will vary from individual to individual. There are Big Dreams and there are Little Dreams. Some dreams have personal meaning and other dreams are universal or archetypal in character.

SSSH, SSSH, SSSH...BE QUIET. HE HAS ALREADY BEGUN HIS LECTURE.

It is against this background that analytic psychology can be understood.

We draw our lives from within the historical universe of which each of us is a part and within which each of us is a whole. It is an archetypal world of living, acting, and influencing individual, psycho-social and collective complexes. The individual psyche consists of a conscious ego, a knowing ego, a personal unconscious, and the collective unconscious.

The personal attitudes of introversion and extroversion unfold within the changing compass of the four psychological functions: thinking, feeling, intuition and sensation.

The developmental cycle of the individual life unfolds within the context of the attraction, opposition, compensation and integration of the static and dynamic polarities of the masculine and feminine.

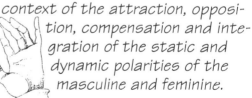

The personality type is a dynamic state of being determined at any one point in time by the conscious and unconscious interaction of the sensate, intuition, thinking and feeling functions.

the shadow side must be revealed

In this process we experience the disintegration of the persona and the consequent collapse of the external world. The evil spirits of our own **shadow** *emerge as real and living beings. We are not who we have pretended to be.*

SHADOW
An unconscious part of the personality characterized by traits that the conscious ego wants to reject or ignore. These 'rejects' of the personality, denied expression in life, coalesce into a fairly autonomous "splinter personality" — the shadow. In dreams, the shadow figure is always of the same sex as the dreamer.

the analysand (the person being psychoanalyzed) is introduced to his/her persona

Perhaps for the first time the analysand is introduced to her/his persona—the social mask behind which each of us hides. The shadow side of our most treasured and valued attributes must be revealed. We are confronted with the unimpeachable fact that the worst of the world's ills lie dormant in our own souls.

PERSONA
(Latin "actor's mask) One's social role, derived from the expectations of society and early training. A strong ego relates to the outside world through a flexible persona; overly strong identification with a specific persona (doctor, scholar, career, etc.) inhibits psychological development.

The maiden anima calls us

The creative power of the maiden anima calls us ever onward into the rich and lasting discovery of our own personhood. But all along the way we split, we resist, we fly from the inevitable terror of our own personal death.

We call upon the spirit of the hero

We call upon the spirit of the hero in our struggle to free ourselves from the unconscious life. But even the invocation of the animus will not wholly contain us. Here in the heart of the darkest night the analyst and analysand must bond together. In that relationship one can sustain the opposites.

The analysand learns to know and love even the most dreaded aspects of the truth. This leads ever onward toward integration and renewal. The individual has indeed died and traveled across the Great Waters to be born again.

In the end the task of analysis is one with the quest of the alchemist—

to create
out of one's own being
an incorruptible substance.

But this analysis is an equally dangerous and potentially explosive process. Here the alchemist's flask is filled with the compounds and elements of the whole of human experience. Just enough energy must be applied. The temperature within the flask must rise but not to the point of exploding beyond its boundaries.

This is a personal experience in which both the analyst and the analysand are equally involved and both are changed in the process. It is a living drama between the forces of good and evil.

The Psychology of Religion

The analytic process moves the analysand from the position of one who acts and reacts to essentially unconscious stimuli into a position of ever increasing consciousness. It is a movement away from the accidents of our own individual history toward an identification with a more transcendent sense of self in which one is identified with God.

The inner life, for Jung, is synonymous with the religious life.

Jung faced a crisis of belief from his earliest days as the first born child of a troubled Protestant minister confronting his own loss of faith and a mother who was too often caught up in the nether world of seances and spiritualism. His earliest dreams and fantasies were filled with the images of the Divine that would later find expression in the world of the "archetype" and of the "**numinous**."

NUMINOUS
It's a tricky concept, best defined indirectly as an offshoot of Animism, the ancient belief that natural things have souls. The numen [the root word of 'numinous'] is the particular spirit [or divinity or god] that inhabits [or presides over] a certain natural object or place. The numinous is a powerful spiritual feeling that (according to Jung and the animists) a sensitive person can feel in the presence of the natural thing or place.

It is the numinous — that presence of the presiding God — that is essential in understanding Jung's psychology of the Self. It is the "Imago Dei" — that mirror reflection of God — that in the final analysis extends beyond the individual ego and whose nature transcends mere human consciousness. It is then this Higher Self that leads the soul or psyche forward toward wholeness.

Although Jung would spend much of his life exploring this central theme as it is expressed in both Western and Eastern religion, he would consistently return to the familiar images of the Christian motif. Indeed he felt that it was essential that Western people come back to the foundations of their own basically Christian tradition. He understood the history of spirituality as a process that evolved through three stages of development which he referred to as the Archaic Period, the Period of Ancient Civilizations and finally and most gloriously the Period of Christianity.

But Jung was not a Christian in the fundamentalist sense of the term. He was a student of the religious and cultural history of mankind which he viewed as a singular process of transformation of the whole of human consciousness. Ultimately this would take on the form of the **quaternity of the mandala** by the means of which both the individual and collective psyche is transformed. It is then this balance, this resolution of duality, that is central to human psychological growth and development as Jung understood it.

| **ARCHAIC PERIOD** (good) | **PERIOD OF ANCIENT CIVILIZATIONS** (better) | **PERIOD OF CHRISTIANITY** (best) |

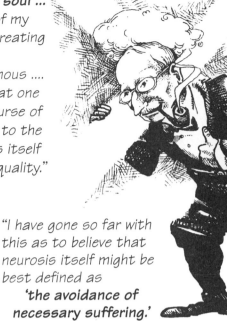

"I am a doctor of the soul ... the primary interest of my work is not in simply treating neuroses but it is in approaching the numinous .... Then to the extent that one becomes free of the curse of illness one can attain to the numinous ... the illness itself takes on a numinous quality." CGJ

"I have gone so far with this as to believe that neurosis itself might be best defined as **'the avoidance of necessary suffering.'**

It is the obvious fact of human suffering that all religions come down to.

But I tell you as Christ Himself told you that 'suffering must be borne.'

If you do not understand this then look to Him!" CGJ

"Now it is important that you understand that as a Christian, I naturally stand on the 'ground of Christian truth.' However, as a psychotherapist I can only go as far with you as the psychological facts will permit me. I have no interest in being converted nor am I interested in converting you." CGJ

the antagonism of opposites

Jung was concerned with the "antagonism of opposites." He searched the pages of history. He studied comparative religion. He traveled to many places and he studied many cultures. All of this in order to deepen his understanding of the problem and the resolution of duality. Western civilization and the modern psyche had become split off from itself. Nowhere was this more apparent for Jung than it is in the formal expression of the modern version of the Christian faith.

maybe, possibly, perhaps, it was rumored...

Jung, it was rumored, was supposed to have been, perhaps, the illegitimate grandson of Johann Wolfgang Goethe. In any event he was very much identified with the problem of Faust who sells his soul to the devil Mephistopheles. And who do you suppose Mephistopheles is? Well, much to the horror of Christian theologians, it turns out to be none other than Jesus Christ himself. The resolution of opposites could not take place without the critical recognition of this fact.

Christ and the Anti-Christ

When you present God as all Goodness and Light, well, what do you suppose happens? Christ then casts a shadow that is all Dark and all Evil. Just who do you suppose that is? Well, that's right, you guessed his name. None other than Mephistopheles, the Devil. Christ and the Anti-Christ are one and the same.

Perhaps you don't think that this is important. If you do not it may be because you have not yet reached that point of consciousness that would enable you to understand that the archetype is a living phenomena with its own specific energy that in fact acts upon the world. The force of evil is real and alive in your universe and mine.

The Blessed Trinity

In order to resolve this unbecoming and troubling psychological and theological dilemma, Jung turned toward the study of early Christian doctrine which much to his delight contained the psychic and historical precedent that he so much longed for. The **Gnostics** of the early Christian church believed not only in the existence of the "Blessed Trinity" (i.e., the Father, the Son, and the Holy Ghost), but also in the existence of a Fourth Force. This was the Force of the Dark Feminine Mysterious Dimension. Something that might be attributed to the residuals of earlier Mother Goddess cultures and maternal religious systems.

GNOSTICS
Early Christian sect(s) that valued inquiry into spiritual matters above faith. They viewed Christ as "non-corporeal" — a spirit without a body — and had other radical ideas. So it's no big surprise that they were usually considered blasphemers by mainstream dogmatic Christians.

YOU SEE, ONCE UPON A TIME NOT SO VERY LONG AGO IN HUMAN HISTORY THE EXPRESSION OF EVEN THE CHRISTIAN FAITH CONTAINED THE FEMININE AS WELL AS THE MASCULINE. THEIRS WAS A FAITH THAT WAS DIFFERENT IN MEANING AND CHARACTER FROM OUR CURRENT OVER-MASCULINIZED EXPRESSION OF PATRIARCHAL DOMINANCE. GOD AS MAN. GOD AS FATHER.

The Fourth Force

What about God as Female?

God as a wholly mas-
culine character
is not the only
way to go. The
Gnostics under-
stood that. And I
might add, much
to their credit,
so do the
Roman
Catholics.

Can you
believe that I
hear myself, a
left-wing
Protestant, say-
ing such a thing?
But it is the truth.
So far as I am con-
cerned the greatest singular religious
event since the Reformation took place in 1950 when Pope Pius
the XII proclaimed the Assumption of Mary, the Mother of God,
into Heaven.

Now this is the part that really cooks my toast. Not only does
she come to heaven to join her son Jesus. She came as His
Celestial Bride. Now, you have just got to know what a hole an
idea like that blows in the minds of most Protestant Fundies.

But you gotta love it, don't you? What Il Papa was saying was that even the whole Freudian Oedipal Complex has its Divine counterpart in the earlier Ascension of Jesus and the later Assumption of his mother Mary. The both arrive in Heaven with their incorruptible human bodies intact!

THIS SOUNDS AN AWFUL LOT LIKE MY PSYCHOANTHROPOLOGY. BUT I THINK YOU'RE GOING OVER THE EDGE WITH THIS STUFF.

The point of the metaphor, the myth, the symbol, the living archetype, of the story of Mary is this: The stuff of the material world, and this, my precious little unconscious ones, includes your own material body, can be raised up into the spiritual world. Before Mary that privilege for the Western mind was reserved only for the masculine.

This Assumption of the Mother of God requires that such a miraculous phenomena be metaphysically anchored in the figure of the wholly Divine Woman.

DIEHARD FEMINISTS IN THE CROWD MAY NOW STAND IN THUNDEROUS APPLAUSE, IF THEY SO DESIRE.

This quest for the resolution of dualities brings Jung to the "Enantiodromania" — the mirror image of the opposites. We humans are on a sacred quest to comprehend "reality," to know "der Wirklichkeit," to find "that which works." The individual as well as the collective psyche gravitates toward what modern systems analysts refer to as "the highest level of organizational invariability." That is to say, we move toward the central organizing principle — the archetype of the transcendent internal life.

Jung contributed much toward opening the way for the Western psyche to approach the exploration of Eastern mythic, spiritual, and religious systems. But he did not do so without reservations. While traveling in India — whether in Borobudor, Bharhut, or Sanchi — he was struck by the wonders of the Indian soul. This was an underworld and an overworld of a purely metaphysical nature out of which emerged "strange forms that became a part of the every-day earthly scene."

What the European mind notices first in India is the outward corporeality that we see everywhere. We Westerners are entirely caught up as it were in the physical world of appearance. We trust what we see and we believe it to be real. But for the Indian soul, life is drawn from the well of Mama Maya — the Mother of Illusions.

This you find most unsettling, do you not? What I am telling you is this. You think you are this. You think you are that. But what you think will tell you nothing of what you want to know.

This reality that you seek is a dream. I am telling you this also. You too are the dream and it is the Great God who is also the Dreamer.

AUM SHANTI

AUM SHANTI

Finally I am telling you this much as well. It is you whom you are seeking and it is you who are the sought. This is the Divine romance in which the Lover becomes the Beloved in the Eternal fact of God as Infinite Love. **(Meher Baba)**

AUM   But why am I telling you this? I am telling you this because I am telling anyone who will listen. But why? Since I am already completely convinced that you Europeans are wholly incapable of hearing.

AUM SHANTI

The spirit of the East is **"ante protas"** — at the door of Western understanding. There might be a healing power within it but there also might be hidden beneath it a dangerous infection. Spiritual Europe will not be helped by a mere sensation. **CGJ**

Yoga will do you no good...

Doing lots of Yoga, standing on your head, might give you some kind of a new thrill, but without the essential ground of thousands of years of the Eastern experience of the soul it will do you no good whatsoever. **CGJ**

Our way must begin in the grounding of our own European reality. What the East has to give can only help in the labor that is already before us. What good is the wisdom of the Upanishads? What good is Yoga if we forsake our own foundations as though they were all mistakes and we had outlived their usefulness. Are we to rapaciously settle on a foreign coast like so many homeless pirates? **CGJ**

According to Jung, the split in the Western mind makes an adequate realization of the intentions of Yoga impossible from the very outset. The Indian, he says, not only knows his nature but knows also to what extent he is that nature. In contrast the European knows astonishingly little about his own nature. Jung recommended that we should study Yoga carefully, but only as an index of Indian spirituality.

Much care should be reserved for the question of whether and to what extent spirituality that has arisen on Eastern soil can be practiced in the West. Jung believed that the West would, over the course of future centuries, produce its own Yoga based on the foundations of Christianity.

Massa Confusa

Our consciousness has borne within it for two thousand years the cultural impulse of the Christ event. This mass importation of exotic religious systems including the Bahai, the Sufis, the Ramakrishna Mission, Buddhism, Theosophy, and Anthroposophy leads only to what the old Alchemists used to refer to as a "Massa Confusa."

Massa the Roman Catholics

...we might actually learn something from the Mass of the Roman Catholics. For all of my interest in Eastern thought, my commitment remains with understanding the Western psyche through a deeper understanding of the symbolic inheritance of the European experience.

One time when I was leaving India in 1937, I had this dream. In it, a voice asked me, "What are you doing in India?" Come to think about it, maybe the voice asked, "What the hell are you doing in India?" The voice went on, "Go find your own urgently needed healing vessel . . . for your state is perilous . . . You," the voice continued, "are in imminent danger of destroying all that the centuries have built up."

. . . I remained in my quarters and buried myself in my Latin alchemical texts. But India did not pass me by without a trace. It left tracks which led from one infinity into another infinity. **CGJ**

Jung never hesitated to recognize hitherto inexplicable facts to which "synchronistic phenomena" also belonged. **Synchronicity** describes a psycho-physical principle that accounts for the fact of coinciding "accidents" or "chance events" which arise from non-rational, non-linear, unconscious "reality." But their simultaneous occurrence is by no means accounted for by either simple chance or mere accident.

Synchronistic Phenomena

egg falls

The irrational fullness of life taught me never to discard anything, even if it went against the tide of existing theories. It is, I must admit, disquieting to question everything. It did not lead to certitude, understand that neither peace nor certainty would lend much to the possibility of new discoveries. **CGJ**

SYNCHRONICITY

A term coined by Jung to designate the "meaningful coincidence" of events that have no precise cause-and-effect relationship to each other. Synchronistic phenomena occur, for instance, when a mental event (dream, vision, premonition, etc.) corresponds to external reality (the premonition or dream "comes true") or when similar thoughts or identical dreams occur at the same time in different places or to different people. These "coincidences" cannot be explained by causality; they seem instead to be connected primarily with activated archetypal processes in the unconscious.

bird lays eggs

Synchronicity

"I have often stood alone with God ..."

Although Jung often stood accused of both Gnosticism and heresy, the existence of God was in his own words "an incontrovertible certainty." His Psychology of Religion was concerned exclusively with the images and concepts which from time immemorial had formed the ineffable being and the very existence of God as the archetype of the Higher Self.

Please, my dear friends, you should not be offended by these "facts" of the psyche that might smooth the way to faith. Belief, however, I must admit is a gift of grace that I like my father before me lost from time to time. But it was this very loss that moved me to seek out the numinous — that of the hidden God within.

I have tried to discover the links between dogma and the immediate experience of the psychological archetype. Not only did I leave the door open to Christianity but I consider it to be of central importance to Western man. **CJG**

I thank God every day that I have been permitted to experience the reality of the "imago Dei" in me. Had it not been so, I would have been a bitter enemy of Christianity and to the Church in particular. Thanks to this "actus gratiae" my life had meaning and my inner eye was opened to the beauty and grandeur of dogma.

Nobody could rob me of the conviction that it was enjoined upon me to do what God wanted and not what I wanted. That gave me the strength to go my own way. Often I had the feeling that in all decisive matters I was no longer among men but was alone with God. **CGJ**

Today too much is at stake and too much obviously depends upon the psychological qualities of man. Is he capable of facing the temptations to make use of his power to bring about the end of the world. . . ? Does he know that he is in peril of losing the life-sustaining myth of the inner man that Christianity . . . has preserved for him . . ? Finally, does he know that it is he who tips the scales . . . has he perceived the Christian message correctly? **CGJ**

**Emma Jung dies
November 27, 1955
Jung age 80**

The Psychology of Alchemy

Jung spent his last years in a continuing search for an historical prefiguration of what he regarded as his own discovery of the psychology of the archetype. Although Herbert Silberer, the Viennese Freudian psychoanalyst, had earlier suggested such an antecedent might be found in the hidden symbolism of alchemy and the occult, it was clearly Jung who would open the doors to this rich psychological treasure house of meaning and metaphor.

According the Jung, Alchemy is related to Christianity in the way that dreams are related to consciousness. Just as the dream compensates in a symbolic fashion for the conflicts of everyday life, so alchemy strives to bring to the surface something of the tensions of opposites that are present beneath the surface of Christianity.

Jung's interest in the study of Alchemy was initially inspired through his association with Richard Wilhelm in Munich. It was 1930 and Jung was 60 years of age. He had written an introduction to Wilhelm's *Secret of the Golden Flower* and in his commentary Jung found the solution to alchemical dream symbology.

Hermes Trismegistus

The European Alchemists of the 15th and 16th centuries, beginning with Hermes Trismegistus, were concerned with turning base metals into gold. They sought a transmuting agent to effect the change. This was the much prized "Lapis" or "philosopher's stone."

Jung would come to understand that profound thinkers among the alchemists were aware that performing the work of the laboratory was only part of their activity. He recognized that the alchemists were trying to express in pseudo-chemical language problems that were primarily spiritual. Therefore they called themselves "philosophers." (translated from *Lovers of Sophia*)

Hermes: *"AURUM NOSTRUM NON EST AURUM VULGI."*

The alchemist's experiences, were in a sense, Jung's experiences — their world became his world. This was of course a momentous discovery. Jung had stumbled upon the historical counterpart of his psychology of the unconscious. He began to understand what the psychic contents of the alchemical texts meant when seen in historical perspective. At last Jung felt that he was no longer alone.

Rosarium Philosophorum

Jung: *"OUR GOLD IS THE THE COMMON GOLD."*

93

Material was mysterious to the alchemists

Whenever we humans confront the unknown, the Unconscious is likely to come into play. Previously unconscious contents make their appearance onto the unknown.

They seem to breathe life into the mystery and make it comprehensible.

WHAT I MUST DO IS START A LEXICON OF KEY PHRASES TO LEARN ABOUT SOME LOST LANGUAGES.

That is precisely what happened to the alchemists. What they encountered as characteristic of matter was in many cases the projected contents of the unconscious. Although it took me quite a while to fully grasp the implications of alchemy-as-unconscious, I had discovered an absolute gold mine of psychic projections.

THAT PROJECT WILL TAKE ME MORE THAN 10 YEARS TO COMPLETE.

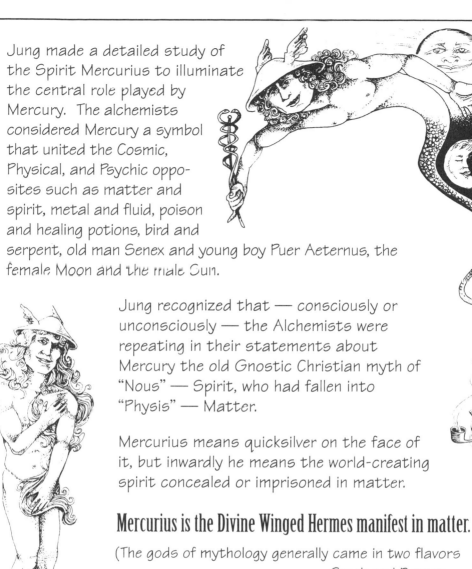

Jung made a detailed study of the Spirit Mercurius to illuminate the central role played by Mercury. The alchemists considered Mercury a symbol that united the Cosmic, Physical, and Psychic opposites such as matter and spirit, metal and fluid, poison and healing potions, bird and serpent, old man Senex and young boy Puer Aeternus, the female Moon and the male Sun.

Jung recognized that — consciously or unconsciously — the Alchemists were repeating in their statements about Mercury the old Gnostic Christian myth of "Nous" — Spirit, who had fallen into "Physis" — Matter.

Mercurius means quicksilver on the face of it, but inwardly he means the world-creating spirit concealed or imprisoned in matter.

Mercurius is the Divine Winged Hermes manifest in matter.

(The gods of mythology generally came in two flavors — Greek and Roman. Mercury is the Roman version, Hermes is the Greek version.)

This the god of revelation, the Lord of Thought and the Sovereign Psychopomp.

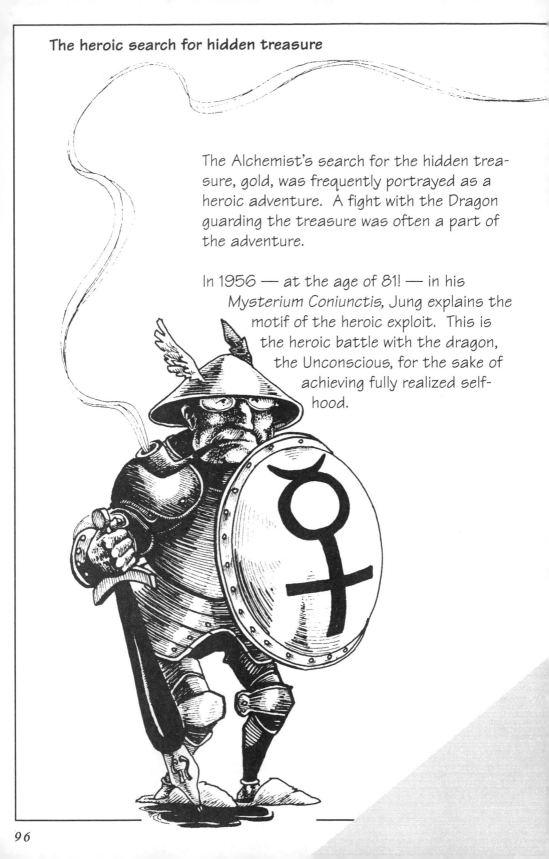

The Alchemist's search for the hidden treasure, gold, was frequently portrayed as a
heroic adventure. A fight with the Dragon
guarding the treasure was often a part of
the adventure.

In 1956 — at the age of 81! — in his
Mysterium Coniunctis, Jung explains the
motif of the heroic exploit. This is
the heroic battle with the dragon,
the Unconscious, for the sake of
achieving fully realized selfhood.

In myths the hero is the one who conquers the Dragon, not the one who is devoured by it, and yet both have to deal with the same Dragon. Also he is no hero who has never met the Dragon, or who if once he saw it, declared afterwards that he saw nothing.

Equally, only one who has risked the fight with the Dragon and is not overcome by it wins the hoard. "The treasure that is hard to attain."

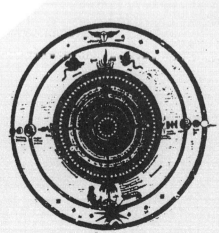

He alone has a genuine claim to self-confidence. For he has faced the dark ground of his own self and thereby has gained himself

He has arrived at an inner certainty which makes him capable of self-reliance and attained what the alchemists called the "unio mentalis."

As a rule this state is represented pictorially by a mandala. *CGJ*

97

Hello there folks, and a pleasant day to you as well, Madama Dragonesa! My name is Marie-Louise Von Franz.

I was just a kid of eighteen when I met our dear mentor, professor and friend Herr Doctor Jung. I got a little bit of a job working for him as a translator after getting my degree in linguistics.

If this part of the story has any kind of a hero or heroine for that matter it has just got to be me. Please forgive me if all of this sounds as though I am lacking in either respect or humility. I am not. I loved the Professor and I still get a kick out of talking about him.

Well anyway, I am the one who suffered through translating so many of those alchemical texts. They were written in Latin and Greek, not German, you will understand.

Anyway when we finally got through all of that I, like so many other of Dr. Jung's female associates, became his patient and analysand.

Then later I went on myself to become a trained analyst and I remained at the Jung Institute in Zurich.

Well anyway, the Professor and I worked out this whole complicated thing that sought to amplify the symbols of analysis as understood by Jungian Analytic Psychologists.

We pored over this book Rosarium Philosophorum in an effort to comprehend the meaning of the Alchemical Marriage. This is a story about how the Gold King marries the Silver Queen. And then, if you can believe it, the two of them die and are reborn as a Siamese-paired Hermaphrodite.

You can only imagine how this sounded to me, an innocent young girl of 18 fresh out of the nest. Well, it gets better. Let me tell you, you ain't heard noth'n yet.

All of this stuff is kind of real "chthonic" like. That means that it is dark, shadowy, and is part of the underground current. I hope that you have learned enough about all of this Jungian opposite stuff to understand that the "chthonic" in life is not so bad as all that.

Even us more ladylike Alchemists believe that there is nothing so evil that good cannot shine forth from within it and there is nothing so good that evil might not be lurking there within it as well.

The analytic process is like jumping into a Mercurial Bath. That's a sort of vessel where the four functions of the personalities of both the Analyst and the Analysand interact. Not at all unlike the chemical process of change.

As the analysis proceeds and we become immersed in the bath of relationship, the Archetype of Wholeness begins to emerge.

Then when everything is just right we move on into the Coniunctio where we are engulfed by the sea. Is this too much or what? That's when a kind of psychic coitus occurs.

Now don't let that get you more fiery types all excited. I would not want you to book passage for Zurich in the vain hope of getting in on some kind of a Dionysian orgy. It's not like that. This is a more subtle kind of process.

Then the Analyst and the Analysand move on through this really ghastly phase of Death and Putrefaction. Most people can deal with the Death part of it, but frankly the Putrefaction part isn't no day at the beach.

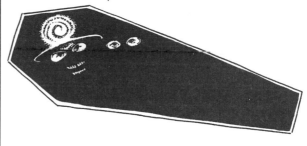

It all turns out nice enough though because the Soul Ascends, is Purified, returns from Heaven, and breathes life into the Hermaphrodite.

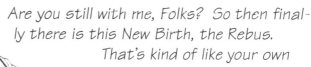

Are you still with me, Folks? So then finally there is this New Birth, the Rebus. That's kind of like your own inner Divine Child being born into the world of your own creation.

The Psychology of Art

The apparent lack of interest in the "art of the insane" during the early period of psychoanalytic development was due to Freud's insistence that, as a method, psychoanalysis was unsuited for work with psychotic patients. Unlike Freud, however, Jung through his affiliation at Burgholzi Hospital had regular access to psychotic patients. He understood early in his career that the psychological processes characteristic of insanity would have provided an additional and particularly valuable means of access to the unconscious.

Dominating my interests and research was the burning question, "What goes on in the mind of the mentally ill?"

The mentally ill, freed from the restrictions of social convention, provided Jung with the opportunity to see deeper into the structure of our common humanity and to penetrate the psyche more deeply than was possible with healthy people. He shared Freud's view that the detailed investigation of pathological phenomena could lead to a more profound understanding of normal psychology. Ebbinghause, whose writings had a great influence upon Jung's choice of careers echoed a similar view:

"Pathological phenomena represent for the understanding of the normal human psychology something similar to the way in which the magnifying glass allows us to see things which are difficult to perceive with the human eye." **Ebbinghause**

"What goes on in the mind of the mentally ill?"

WHAT'S THIS HERE—A PICTURE? CRAZY LOOKING SORT OF A THING BUT I KNOW IT MEANS SOMETHING. I'VE SEEN THIS SAME SORT OF THING SOMEWHERE ELSE.

Freud had earlier suggested that the normal individual is made psychotic by sleep. What we are faced with here is an ancient but extinct mode of expression that was initially non-verbal. Communication was perhaps wholly by means of symbols and visualizations. This "atavistic" tendency to reflect the art of earlier periods of human history lead to Freud's "theory of phylogenetic heritage." Jung was one of Freud's few analytic followers who believed with him that even particular psychical contents such as symbolism have no source other than hereditary transmission.

Both men in the name of science were proclaiming that we human beings are capable of making symbolic connections never acquired by learning — that we have a collective Phylogenetic Heritage.

Hi folks, this is Uncle Siggy speaking! Now I understand that by this point in the story I am already dead but this part makes me raise right up out of the grave.

Yes, Jung and I both agree on the phylogenetic stuff. Of course I agree. It was my idea for heaven's sake. But these Jungian types, they go right off the edge with this stuff. Everything according to them has a "collective unconscious" solution. Everything the patient dreams about is supposed to be drawn out of our common symbolic heritage. But my dears,

before we choose the "phylogenetic" answer, we ought first to look for the more obvious "ontogenetic" answer.

That is a fancy way of saying that for both the psychotherapist and the aestheticist, we must thoroughly exhaust what we can know about the patient or the artist's real life experience in the real world. Then perhaps we can generalize something further — but not before!

...that having been said, perhaps I can rest a bit more peacefully!

From his own experience of madness...

Jung knew and understood from his own experience of madness the value of grounding the image through drawing and painting. This use of the symbolic enabled him to transcend his own delusions and to make his way back out of his nightmare of the psychosis. He was responsive for the rest of his life to the representations of the unconscious.

THE SHADOW PERSONIFIES EVERYTHING THAT WE DO NOT WISH TO ACKNOWLEDGE ABOUT OURSELVES.

The Jung Institute in Zurich houses a picture archive that incorporates case histories, paintings, and drawings of numerous patients, including psychotics. Jung's followers have continued to add to the storehouse of dream interpretation and the images drawn from the depths of our individual and collective psychic experience. It was however Dr. Jolande Jacobi whose work provided the most extensive review of Jungian thinking about patient art and its interpretation. Dr. Angela Jaffe would later expand Jung's influence to include symbolism in the visual arts.

OUR BELOVED HERR PROFESSOR DOKTOR JUNG PROVIDED US WITH THE INSPIRATION AND THE MOTIVATION TO SEE IN THE TWISTED AND TROUBLED MINDS OF THE MENTALLY ILL THE VERY SYMBOLS OF TRANSFORMATION OFTEN CURIOUSLY LACKING IN THE WORK OF THE SO-CALLED SANE ARTIST.

YES, AND WHAT IS MORE IS THAT THE UNCONSCIOUSNESS IS THE SOURCE OF NUMINOUS IMAGES AND SYMBOLS THAT HAVE THE POWER TO CHANGE US.

THE ARTIST ALLOWS US TO ACCOMPANY HER ON THE HEROIC JOURNEY INTO THE REALMS OF THE UNCONSCIOUS. THE UNREASONED, THE ILLOGICAL. WE EMERGE FROM THE ENCOUNTER OFTEN DISTURBED BUT WE EMERGE INTACT.

AFTER I WAS THROWN OUT OF GERMANY FOR BEING JEWISH, I WAS WELCOMED TO SWITZERLAND BY DR. JUNG.

Dr. Jolande Jacobi

Dr. Angela Jaffe

BUT THERE ARE THOSE WHO WILL NOT — WHO CANNOT — RETURN FROM THE MAGIC KINGDOM OR THE MADNESS OF HELL. THEY CAN ONLY SHARE WITH US THEIR VISIONS AND IMAGES. BUT IN THEIR MADNESS THEY REVEAL TO US A COMMON REALITY THAT LIES HIDDEN BENEATH THE VENEER OF CONVENTION.

ANGI, PERHAPS YOU MIGHT RECALL A COMMENT BY LIZA DOOLITTLE WHOM OUR AUDIENCE WILL REMEMBER AS MY FAIR LADY. "THE DIFFERENCE," SHE SAID, "BETWEEN A LADY AND A FLOWER GIRL IS NOT WHO SHE IS, BUT HOW YOU TREAT HER." THE SAME THING MIGHT BE SAID OF THE ARTIST AND THE MADMAN.

JAFFEJOLI, I COULDN'T AGREE WITH YOU MORE. BUT LOOK OVER THERE. ISN'T THAT ERICH NEUMAN? ERICH, ERICH, OVER HERE, HONEY!

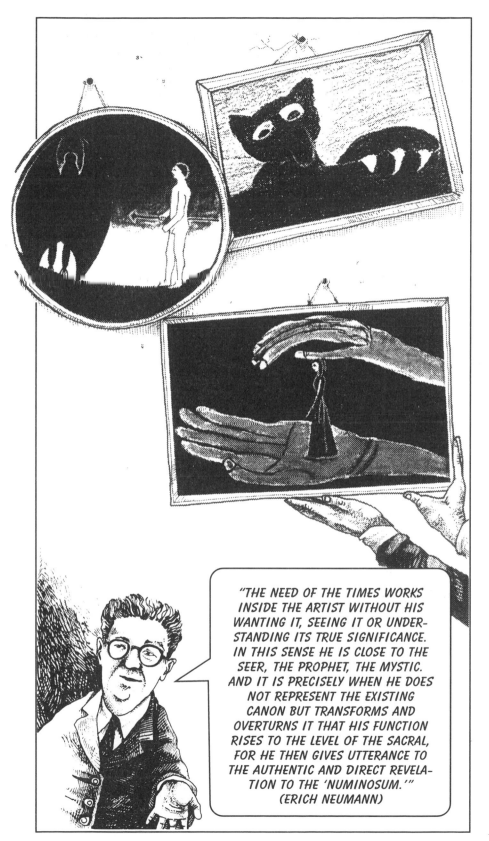

"THE NEED OF THE TIMES WORKS INSIDE THE ARTIST WITHOUT HIS WANTING IT, SEEING IT OR UNDERSTANDING ITS TRUE SIGNIFICANCE. IN THIS SENSE HE IS CLOSE TO THE SEER, THE PROPHET, THE MYSTIC. AND IT IS PRECISELY WHEN HE DOES NOT REPRESENT THE EXISTING CANON BUT TRANSFORMS AND OVERTURNS IT THAT HIS FUNCTION RISES TO THE LEVEL OF THE SACRAL, FOR HE THEN GIVES UTTERANCE TO THE AUTHENTIC AND DIRECT REVELATION TO THE 'NUMINOSUM.'" (ERICH NEUMANN)

The Psychology of Sexuality

Sigmund Freud under-took the clinical case studies that led to his formulations of psychoanalysis in the second half of the 1800's. This was a world where the sexes were rigidly divided by definition and sex role stereotypes. Men were men and women were women.

Those who consulted Doctor Freud were people who often suffered physical symptoms that had no apparent organic basis. Eventually Freud came to believe that most of these hysterical manifestations had their origin in repressed sexual problems especially associated with the traumatic experiences of early childhood.

The sexual impulse was to become the central interpretative principle of psychoanalysis. Freud predicated the most important tenets of his theoretical formulations on the biological basis of human sexual behavior.

"Anatomy," he proclaimed, "is destiny!"

At the center of Freud's theory was the concept of human bisexuality. Freud however did not arrive at these formulations alone. During the transitional years between the estrangement from his mentor Dr. Joseph Breuer and the completion of his own "self analysis," he became the best of friends with Wilhelm Fliess, a nose and throat specialist from Berlin who was two years his junior.

Many writers have commented on the great passion that Freud expressed for Fliess, even subtly hinting at the existence of homosexual overtones in their relationship. Speaking of one of their not infrequent two or three day meetings together, Freud wrote that he "panted for it as to a slaking of hunger and thirst." After spending these times together Freud said that he felt himself "in a state of continual euphoria and working like a youth."

Freud himself described his time with Fliess as

"A PROPER WISH FULFILLMENT, A BEAUTIFUL DREAM.... I HAVE BEEN NEWLY FORTIFIED FOR WEEKS, NEW IDEAS PRESSED FORWARD, PLEASURE IN THE HARD WORK WAS RESTORED, AND THE FLICKERING HOPE OF FINDING ONES WAY THROUGH THE JUNGLE BURNED FOR A WHILE STEADILY AND BRILLIANTLY." FREUD

HOLD IT! HOLD IT! CUT! STOP THE SHOW!

I'm sorry to interrupt you boys but you have not yet completed your homework. This is "but another example of the fact that just because an argument is convincing it does not necessarily mean that it is right."

"More recent comparative embryology had added some new information that makes obsolete the traditional psychoanalytic concepts that suggest the inferiority of female sexuality!" (Singer)

The early embryo is <u>not</u> bisexual, as Freud, Jung and the rest of the boys thought. It is <u>not</u> so undifferentiated.

"IT" IS FEMALE!

"Although modern biologists are now aware that we were all female at the beginning, it will probably be a long time before the influence of these discoveries filters down to the level where theologians will be ready to consider an 'Adam-out-of-Eve' version of Genesis." (Singer)

Dr. June Singer

ALL

WE ARE WOMAN

ALL RIGHT LADIES, ON YOUR FEET. LET'S HEAR IT FOR OUR SIDE. MUCH APPLAUSE, PLEASE.

OH, WHO ME? I'M JUNE SINGER, THE EMINENT PSYCHOLOGIST, DOCTOR, AND TRAINED JUNGIAN ANALYST. MEANWHILE, BACK TO FREUD AND THE NOSE DOCTOR...

According to Frank Sulloway writing in Freud, Biologist of the Mind (1992), Freud's buddy Fliess-the-nose-doctor believed that some nasal conditions in women were due to "reflex neurosis." All such disorders according to Freud's eminent colleague, arise from two principle sources: organic disturbances of the nose, and vasomotor (functional) disturbances associated with the female reproductive system. He assumed a special physiological link between the nose and the genitalia, an association he localized within certain "genital spots" inside the interior of the nose.

On the basis of this purported "nasalgenital" link, Freud would refer some of his female patients to Fliess for his nasal surgeries undertaken (with cocaine of course) to cure painful intercourse and other forms of Dyspareunia.

HEY SIGGY, REMEMBER THAT OLD MEDICAL SCHOOL JOKE? "DYSPAREUNIA IS BETTER THAN NO PAREUNIA AT ALL." DID YOU EVER HEAR ANYTHING SO FUNNY IN ALL YOUR LIFE?

Dr. June Singer, in her definitive exposition *Androgyny: The Opposites Within*, presents a comparative analysis of Freud's and Jung's theories of human sexuality. Freud pioneered an original and daring theory of sexuality and presented it as a rational system in terms of the scientific thinking of his time. Jung, although equally committed to the biology of human bisexuality, was less bound by rational considerations and was able to carry the concept of our inner female and maleness to the symbolic level.

Separating Sex and Gender

According to Dr. Singer, Jung did not get caught in the trap of "biological bisexuality" to the degree that Freud did. He was able to break new ground when he separated the concepts of sex and gender, enabling him to see the Masculine as apart from maleness and the Feminine as apart from femaleness.

The **Masculine**, as apart from maleness, he saw as the **"Animus"** in women.

The **Feminine**, as apart from femaleness, he saw as **"Anima"** in men.

It is on account of this formulation, made in his early years, that Jung has received so much criticism from those striving for equalization of opportunity, and status as human beings between the two sexes. Both Freud and Jung made specific characterizations of what it is to be "masculine" and what it is to be "feminine."

Each of these men were spokesmen for the times and the cultures in which they lived. Both Freudian psychoanalysts and Jungian analytic psychologists have often served to promote the ideas of the culture in power at the moment. **(Singer)**

WOMEN IN SWITZERLAND WON THE RIGHT TO VOTE IN 1971.

Robert Hopcke, writing in *Jung, Jungians and Homosexuality*, for example, points out that the appearance of the over-determined anima in a man was generally looked down on by Jung and his followers.

A man's "femininity" was usually considered the result of some negative projection of the Mother Complex, while the "animus bound" woman was possessed of some dark "Father Complex."

"The mental masculinization of the woman has unwelcome results.

She may perhaps be a good comrade to a man without having access to his feelings. The reason is that her animus — not true reasonableness — has stopped up the approaches to her own feelings.

She may even become frigid..."

Jung, however, came to the defense of homosexuals in Germany.

In 1929 he wrote:

THE YOUNG ARE EXPERIMENTING LIKE YOUNG DOGS. THEY WANT TO LIVE EXPERIMENTALLY, WITH NO HISTORICAL PREMISES. THAT CAUSES REACTIONS IN THE UNCON-SCIOUS, RESTLESSNESS AND LONGING FOR FULFILLMENT...BUT THE YOUNG TODAY CAN BE FORBIDDEN NO STUPIDITIES..."

Earlier, in 1914, he wrote:

"HOMOSEXUALITY WOULD BE A TREMENDOUS ADVANTAGE SINCE MANY INFERIOR MEN WHO WOULD QUITE REASON-ABLY LIKE TO REMAIN ON THE HOMOSEXUAL LEVEL, ARE NOW FORCED INTO MARRIAGE.

HAVE YOU EVER CONSIDERED THE LATENCY PROBLEM? HOW ABOUT ARRESTED DEVELOPMENT?

IT, HOMOSEXUALITY, WOULD ALSO BE EXCELLENTLY SUITED TO LARGE AGGLOMERATIONS OF MALES. (BUSINESSES, UNIVERSITIES)

BECAUSE OF OUR SHORT-SIGHTED-NESS, WE FAIL TO RECOGNIZE THE BIOLOGICAL SERVICES RENDERED BY HOMOSEXUAL SEDUCERS. ACTUALLY THEY SHOULD BE CRED-ITED WITH SOMETHING OF THE SANCTITY OF MONKS." CGJ

Carl Jung, unlike Freud, did not formulate a specific theory of human sexuality. It has been suggested that his failure to do so was as least partially a compensatory response to Freud's "overly sexualized" theory of human psychological development. But his interest in religion, alchemy, and the other historical antecedents of his theory of the collective unconscious opened the door to an androgynous understanding of the human psyche.

The rise of Women's Liberation, Gay Liberation, the continuing influence of the humanistic ego analysts, and a more integrated approach to our current understanding of the biology and psychology of sexuality has done much to change all of this in both the Freudian and Jungian camps.

Hopcke recalls that it was Jung who suggested the alchemical Hermaphrodite, a two-sided sexual being, as emblematic of spiritual wholeness. To a large measure it has been in the tradition of C.G. Jung that we have begun to explore the role, for example, of the Native American "berdache," to broaden our understanding of same-sex relationships.

"THE IDEA THAT SEXUAL ORIENTATION EMERGES FROM A COMPLEX INTERACTION OF THE PERSONAL AND ARCHETYPAL MASCULINE, FEMININE AND ANDROGYNE GIVES ONE A DEEPER AND CLEARER VISION OF THE INNER LIVES OF BOTH HOMOSEXUAL AND HETEROSEXUAL MEN AND WOMEN IN WESTERN CULTURES...

THUS ACCORDING EACH INDIVIDUAL THE POTENTIAL WHOLENESS THAT LIES SYMBOLICALLY AND EMOTIONALLY IN A PRIMARY EROTIC RELATIONSHIP." (HOPCKE)

Improved Human Relations

On the surface, Jung's suggestions toward a theory of psycho-sexual development may not appear that radically different from Freud's. Both men's ideal might be characterized simply as "improved human relations." And Jung, like his mentor, understood that the ego functioned as a mediator between the unconscious elements of the psyche and the demands of the external world.

But there was a difference.

For Jung, the ego revolved around a higher concept of the Self, closer perhaps to Freud's later notions of Libidinal Energy.

Like "a circle whose center is everywhere and whose circumfer-ence is nowhere."

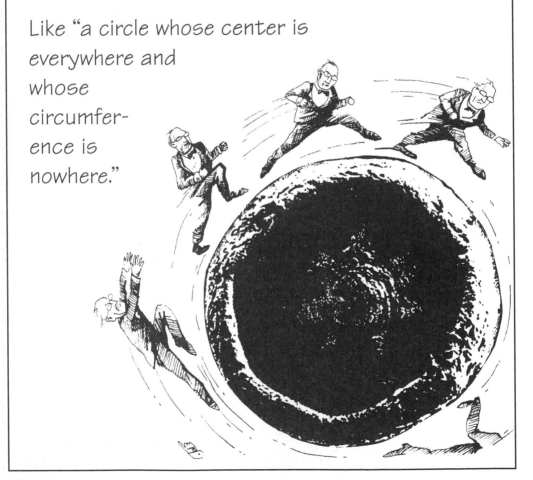

The archetype of the androgyne, according to Singer, is "a symbol of the Self par excellence." This is a representation in human form of the principle of wholeness. Out of the sexual union of man and woman, each of us is born of the maternal wellspring of all creation — each individual being born with their own unique genetic code of DNA molecules.

Singer:

BUT TO SAY THAT THE ANDROGYNE IS ONLY A CERTAIN TYPE OF PERSON IS TO MISS JUNG'S POINT ENTIRELY.

ANDROGYNE IS THE OUTCOME OF A DYNAMISM BASED ON THE APPLICATION OF ENERGY IN AN ORGANIC SYSTEM THAT IS OPEN-ENDED AND THAT IS INTERFACED WITH AN OPEN-ENDED UNIVERSE.

THE ANDROGYNE IS HERE. THE ANDROGYNE IS PRESENT IN EACH PERSON. "HOW SHALL I DESCRIBE THE ANDROGYNE?

IT IS HARD TO DESCRIBE A FEELING THAT IS SO MUCH THE ESSENCE OF ONES BEING THAT ONE IS SCARCELY AWARE OF IT.

IT IS AS IF THE MOLECULES OF ONE'S BEING WERE DANCING TOGETHER WITHOUT TOUCHING.

The Age of Pisces has passed. The Age of Aquarius is upon us.

*"To some this may come as a new idea.
To others it is as old as the mystical dance
of the man-woman-Lord, Shiva . . .*

Nataraja

Om Namah
Shivaya

Sivaya
Namah Om

. . . who moved in the Fiery Circle
of process
as Destroyer of what was old
and had been presented too long.

Toward the primordial chaos
from which new creation springs."

Jaya Siva

Comments From Another Dimension

So at this point I thought that I might as well take this show right over the top. I thought I should close with a few thoughtful comments on UFOs. These so-called "unidentified flying objects" could very well be messengers from some other dimension.

ARE THESE SIGNALS COMING FROM SOME OTHER HIGHER CONSCIOUSNESS OF TIME AND OF SPACE?

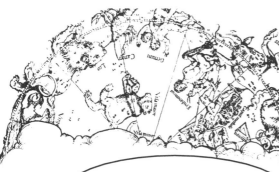

IS SYNCHRONICITY MEANINGFUL? DO SO-CALLED CHANCE EVENTS REFLECT AN ORDERED COSMIC CONSCIOUSNESS? IF SO, IS THIS ORDERED COSMIC CONSCIOUSNESS ACCESSIBLE TO OUR COLLECTIVE PSYCHE?

IS THERE A TRANSCENDENT MEANING THAT GOES BEYOND INDIVIDUAL CONSCIOUSNESS?

CAN WE DENY THAT THERE IS SOMETHING ETERNAL IN ALL OF THIS?

THIS MIGHT SEEM TOO FAR OUT FOR SOME OF US, BUT FOR OTHERS THE MIND HAS OPENED TO LARGER POSSIBILITIES.

WE CAN LEARN TO HEAR MESSAGES FROM THE OTHER SIDE.

Jung believed in immortality.
He urged us to fearlessly embrace our fate.

"THE FEAR OF FATE IS A VERY UNDERSTANDABLE PHENOMENA, FOR IT
IS INCALCULABLE, IMMEASURABLE, FULL OF UNKNOWN DANGERS."

"THE PERPETUAL HESITATION OF THE NEUROTIC TO LAUNCH OUT INTO
LIFE IS READILY EXPLAINED BY HIS DESIRE TO STAND ASIDE SO AS NOT
TO GET INVOLVED IN THE DANGEROUS STRUGGLE FOR EXISTENCE."

"BUT ANYONE WHO REFUSES TO EXPERIENCE LIFE MUST STIFLE HIS
DESIRE TO LIVE." CGJ

Jung believed in immortality and in things immortal.
He was in the end an optimist who urges us to fearlessly embrace our fate.

"BUT LIKE A PROJECTILE FLYING TO ITS GOAL, LIFE MUST END IN DEATH. EVEN ITS ASCENT AND ITS ZENITH ARE ONLY STEPS AND MEANS TO THIS END."

"IN THE SECRET HOUR OF LIFE'S MIDDAY THE PARABOLA IS REVERSED, DEATH IS BORN. THE SECOND HALF OF LIFE DOES NOT SIGNIFY... ASCENT... UNFOLD-ING... EXUBERANCE... BUT DEATH, SINCE THE END IS ITS GOAL."

LIFE MUST END IN DEATH...

"THE BIRTH OF A HUMAN BEING IS PREGNANT WITH MEANING, SO WHY NOT DEATH? THE HIGHEST SUMMIT OF LIFE CAN BE BEST EXPRESSED IN THE SYMBOLISM OF DEATH. CGJ

"Yes, I do believe in the immortal. I know that the psyche is pre-existent to consciousness. The impor-tant question is not "What happens to us after we die?" But rather, "Where were we before we were born?" (JP)

127

Carl Gustav Jung as we have seen was and to a large extent remains a seminal figure. It seems at times that he was larger than life. He was also a man who considered the fate and the fact of his own and our own death.

A man should be able to say he has done his best to form a conception of life after death, or to create some image of it — even if he must confess failure. Not to have done so is a vital loss. Not only my own dreams but the dreams of others, helped to shape, revise, or confirm my views of a life after death.

If there is consciousness after death, it would, so it seems to me, have to continue on the level of consciousness attained by humanity.

Buddha was twice asked by his disciples whether man's karma is personal or not. Each time he fended off the question...considering it better that his disciples meditate upon birth, life, old age and death and upon the cause of suffering.

I know no answer to the question of whether the karma which I live is the outcome of my past lives.... Have I lived before in the past as a specific personality....Buddha left the question open, and I like to assume that he himself did not know with certainty.

As far as we can discern — in the here and now — the sole purpose of human existence is to kindle a light in the darkness of mere being. **CGJ**

For CG Jung that light would continue to burn brightly well into his eighties. At 81 years of age in 1957, Jung's biography would be recorded and edited by Angela Jaffe in *Memories, Dreams and Reflections*. This was followed in 1958 by *Ein Moderner Mythus* (Flying Saucers: A Modern Myth). Then in 1961 at the age of 85 he finished his last work *Approaching the Consciousness in Man and His Symbols*.(1964)

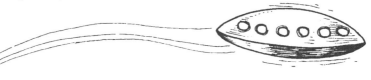

After a short illness, Carl Gustav Jung died on June 6, 1961 in his house on the lake at Kusnacht, Switzerland. He was 85 years old. The inscription on his tombstone reads:

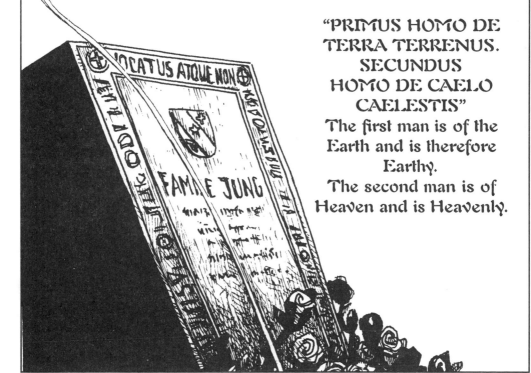

"VOCATUS ATQUE NON VOCATUS DEUS ADERIT."
Summoned or not God shall be there.

"PRIMUS HOMO DE TERRA TERRENUS. SECUNDUS HOMO DE CAELO CAELESTIS"
The first man is of the Earth and is therefore Earthy.
The second man is of Heaven and is Heavenly.

Here we find ourselves, you and I, in another dimension where we might have met before and where we might meet again. But for now, won't you join me and my fellow players

Join with us,
saints and sinners all,
until we meet again.

"You are one
and we are one
and we are all together.

Appendix

Chapter Notes

When the letters **"CGJ"** appear, this means that Jung is being quoted directly. At other times we are paraphrasing our understanding of what Jung might have said in this context. Sources are referenced in Chapter Notes.

Carl Jung, The Life

Many of the source materials available on Carl Jung have been written quite naturally by his followers and those who admired his work. We have called upon the same sources. Gerhard Wehr's <u>Jung A Biography</u> (1987)and Vincent Brome's <u>Jung Man & Myth</u> (1978) present in-depth and scholarly biography.

<u>Memories Dreams and Reflections</u> written by Jung and edited by Angela Jaffe (1961), presents the personal reflections of Jung's life which would end shortly after its completion.

Angela Jaffe's more recent <u>CG Jung Word and Image</u> (1979), together with Gerhard Wehr's highly illustrated <u>CG Jung</u> (1989), are filled with original photographs and documents that bring the life and times of Jung to our eyes.

These sources have provided much of the material in Chapter 1, "Mothers, Fathers, Saints and Sinners" and Chapter 3, "Jung's Dark Night of the Soul."

This material has been balanced by writings on Jung that come from outside the Jungian camp. Most notable in this regard are Peter Gay's definitive <u>Freud - A Man For Our Times</u> (1988) and Duane Schutz' <u>Intimate Friends, Dangerous Rivals</u> "The Turbulent Relationship between Freud and Jung." (1990)

Jerry Diller's <u>Freud's Jewish Identity</u> "A Case Study in the Impact of Ethnicity" (1991) was instrumental in our presentation of Freud. This work was further considered in <u>Lingering Shadows</u> "Jungians, Freudians, and Anti-Semitism," a CG Jung Foundation book, 1991.

The story of Sabina Spielrein is told from her own recollections as presented by John Kerr in <u>A Most Dangerous Method</u> (1994) and by Aldo Carotenuto in <u>A Secret Symmetry</u> "The Untold Story of the Woman Who Changed the Early History of Psychoanalysis." (1983)

These sources provided much of the information conveyed in Chapter 2, "Jung, Freud, Intimacy and Betrayal" and Chapter 4, "Jung, Freud, and the Holocaust." More specific reference is made by author in the text. Robert Hopcke's <u>A Guided Tour of the Collected Works of CG Jung</u> (1989) provides a valuable resource in approaching Jung's work directly. Hopcke presents a guide to the collective works divided into four major headings of interest: - Part 1: "The Ways and Means of the Psyche," Part 2: "Archetypal Figures," Part 3: "Topics of Interest," and Part 4: "Esoterica." This direct source served to inform the whole of <u>Jung for Beginners.</u>

Carl Jung, The Work

Chapter 5, "The Foundations of Jungian Psychology," Chapter 6, "The Structure of the Psyche," and Chapter 9, "Jungian Analytic Psychology" have been largely informed by Ira Progoff's very readable <u>Jung's Psychology</u> "And Its Social Meaning" (1973), Murry Stein's edition of <u>Jungian Analysis</u> (1982) and Michael Fordham's <u>Jungian Psychotherapy</u> (1978).

Less accessible sources to these chapters have included Jolande Jacobi's <u>The Way of Individuation</u> (1967) and CG Jung's <u>The Practice of Psychotherapy</u> "Essays on the Psychology of Transference and Other Subjects" (1954). Stephen Segalles and Merril Berger's <u>The Wisdom of the Dream,</u> a CG Jung Foundation book (1990), provided much of the interpretation included in the section under the same title in Chapter 9.

Chapter 7, "Personality Types," draws from Progoff cited above as well as Jung's Typology by Marie-Louise von Franz and James Hillman (1979). Psychological Types by CG Jung served as a direct source, Bollingen Series, (1976).

The current major interest in the application of Jungian typology has been cited in our inclusion of the Myers-Briggs typology as referenced in Gifts Differing by Isabel Briggs-Myers (1980) and Please Understand Me by David Keirsey and Marilyn Bates (1987). The reader is referred to the Center for the Application of Psychological Type and to the Consulting Psychology Press in Palo Alto, California for further information.

Chapter 8, "The Dynamic of the Archetype" is drawn from the work of Gareth Hill in Masculine and Feminine (1992). He builds upon Erick Neumann's interpretation of Jung's basic identification of the masculine and feminine principles.

Hill reminds us that an understanding of this chapter, as might be said of Jung in general, requires both linear and non-linear thinking. That is to say, here we must learn by using both the rational and non-rational approaches to learning.

James Hillman's brief account of archetypal psychology is also recommended as an overview of the information included in this section. Sallie Nichols' Jung and the Tarot "An Archetypal Journey" introduced by Laurens van der Post (1980) presents an interesting application of Jung's theory.

Chapters 10 and 11 "The Psychology of Religion" and "The Psychology of Art" draw heavily from sources cited in the first section: Jung, The Life. Other indirect sources include Edward Edinger's Ego and the Archetype; "Individuation and the Religious Function of the Archetype."

In these chapters perhaps somewhat more than in others we have also turned directly to Jung. Reference includes The Undiscovered Self, Vol. 10 (1958), Psychology and Religion, Vol. 11 (1958), and Yoga and the West, Vol 11 (1958). The work of Jung's introductions to others were also illuminating. Notable in this regard were: Psychological Commentary on The Tibetan Book of Great Liberation, edited by Evans-Wentz (1954) and Richard Wilhelm's Commentary on the Secret Flower and his forward to The I Ching (1950).

Chapter 12 "The Psychology of Art" makes reference to John Mac Gregor's The Art of the Insane produced by Princeton University Press (1989). Jung's scathing review of Picasso and its relationship to Jung's involvement in the politics of Nazi Germany is cited earlier in Chapter 4, Jung Freud and the Holocaust (see MacGregor, page 237-243). Our view is further influenced by Erich Neumann's Art and the Creative Unconscious (1959). Reference was made to the works of Marie-Louise von Franz, Joseph Henderson, Jolande Jacobi, and Angela Jaffe as they appear in Jung's Man and His Symbols (1964).

Chapter 13, "The Psychology of Sexuality" is drawn almost exclusively from the ideas and comments of June Singer writing in Androgyny "The Opposites Within" (1989). Her formulations of Jung's thinking on human sexuality were further informed by Robert Hopcke's Jung, Jungians and Homosexuality.

The material on Fliess, the biologist, is based on research in Frank J. Sulloway's Freud, Biologist of the Mind, "Beyond the Psychoanalytic Legend," Harvard, (1992).

Chapter 14, "Comments From Another Dimension," draws from the whole of the material cited above. However it is particularly informed by Jung's The Undiscovered Self cited above and CG Jung Psychological Reflections "A New Anthology of His Writing 1905-1961," edited by Jolande Jacobi and R.F.C. Hull, Bollingen Series, Princeton (1978).

The questions raised in this section and Jung's reflections on life and death are largely drawn from his own words.

Glossary

ALCHEMY

The older form of chemistry, which combined experimental chemistry in the modern sense with general, symbolic, intuitive, quasi-religious speculations about nature and man. Onto the unknown <u>materia</u> were projected many symbols which we now recognize as contents of the unconscious. The alchemist was said to pursue the secret and the method of turning material into gold. The alchemist also was seeking the "secret of God" in the unknown substance and thereby embarked on procedures and paths of exploration which resemble those of the modern-day psychology of the unconscious. This science, too, finds itself confronted with an unknown objective phenomenon—the unconscious.

ANALYTIC PSYCHOLOGY

The study and application of Jung's idea of the psyche and its processes through the dynamics of the transference experienced by the analysand with the analyst.

ANIMA and ANIMUS

Personification of the feminine nature of a man's unconscious and the masculine nature of a woman's. This psychological bisexuality is a reflection of the biological fact that it is the larger number of male (or female) genes which is the decisive factor in the determination of sex. The smaller number of contrasexual genes seems to produce a corresponding contrasexual character, which usually remains unconscious. Anima and animus manifest themselves most typically in personified form as figures in dreams and fantasies ("dream girl," "dream lover"), or in the irrationalities of a man's <u>feeling</u> and a woman's <u>thinking</u>. As regulators of behavior they are two of the most influential archetypes. Anima: (Latin "soul") Unconscious feminine side of the psyche; (in classical Jungian Psychology) of the male personality. Animus: (Latin "spirit") Unconscious masculine side of the psyche; (in classical Jungian Psychology) of the female personality. Later Jungians including many of the author's cited, have defined the archetype in broader contrasexual language. The psyches of both women and men include the archetypes of the anima and the animus.

ARCHETYPE
Universal patterns or motifs which come from the collective unconscious and are the basic content of religions, mythologies, legends, and fairytales; emerging in individuals in the form of dreams, visions and fantasies. The archetype carries specific energy and is capable of acting upon the world.

ASSOCIATION
A spontaneous flow of interconnected thoughts and images around a specific idea, determined by unconscious connections. Jung's earlier work at Burgholzli Hospital on word association used by Freud as "free association."

COMPLEX
An emotionally charged group of ideas and/or images; at the center of which is an archetype or archetypal image.

CONSCIOUSNESS
C.G.JUNG. "When one reflects upon what consciousness really is, one is profoundly impressed by the extreme wonder of the fact that an event which takes place outside in the cosmos simultaneously produces an internal image, that it takes place, so to speak, inside as well, which is to say: becomes conscious."

CONSTELLATE
Whenever there is a strong emotional and/or psychic reaction to a person, situation, or psychosocial environment, a 'complex' has been 'constellated.' (activated or triggered)

DREAM

C.G. JUNG: "The dream is a little hidden door in the innermost and most secret recesses of the soul, opening into that cosmic night which was psyche long before there was any ego-consciousness, and which will remain psyche no matter how far our ego-consciousness extends....It is from the all-uniting depths that the dream arises, be it never so childish, grotesque, and immoral....Dreams are neither deliberate nor arbitrary fabrications; they are natural phenomena which are nothing other than what they pretend to be. They do not deceive, they do not lie, they do not distort or disguise, but naively announce what they are and what they mean."

EGO

The central complex in the field of consciousness. A strong ego can relate objectively to activated contents of the unconscious (other complexes), rather than identifying with them. Jung believed in this lower self (based on experience) and in a Higher Self which is to be differentiated from the ego and is to be identified with God.

FEELING

One of the four "functions" of the psyche. In Jungian terms it is regarded as a "rational" evaluation. In general the term in "recovery" language would address an actual bodily reaction to a given stimuli which might have been previously denied as a consequence of ego defense.

INDIVIDUATION

The conscious realization of one's unique psychological reality, including both strengths and limitations. It leads to the experiencing of the Self as the regulating center of the psyche. C.G.JUNG: "I use the term 'individuation' to denote the process by which a person becomes a psychological 'in-divid-ual,' that is, a separate, indivisible unity or 'whole.'"

138

"Individuation means becoming an 'in-dividual,' and in so far as 'individuality' embraces our innermost, last, and incomparable uniqueness, it also implies becoming one's own self. We could therefore translate individuation as 'coming to selfhood' or 'self-realization.'"

"But again and again I note that the individuation process is confused with the coming of the ego into consciousness and that the ego is in consequence identified with the self, which naturally produces a hopeless conceptual muddle. Individuation is then nothing but ego-centeredness and auto-eroticism. But the self comprises infinitely more than a mere ego...It is as much one's self, and all other selves, as the ego. Individuation does not shut one out from the world, but gathers the world to oneself.."

INFLATION
A state in which one has either an unrealistically high or low sense of identity. It indicates a regression of consciousness into unconsciousness which typically happens when the ego takes too many unconscious contents upon itself and loses the faculty of discrimination.

INTUITION
One of the four "Functions" of Jungian typology. It stands in contrast to Sensation function and enables the ego to "know" by way of the ;unconscious. (located in the corpus collosum of the human brain, which is incidentally larger in women than in men).

NEUROSIS
State of being at odds with oneself, caused by the conflict between instinctive drives and the demands of one's society, between infantile obstinacy and the desire to conform, between collective and individual obligations. Neurosis is a stop sign marking a wrong turning, a summons to be cured. CG JUNG: "The inability to accept necessary suffering....Neurosis is always a substitute for legitimate suffering."

NUMINOSUM
Rudolf Otto's term (Idea of the Holy) for the inexpressible, mysterious, terrifying, directly experienced and pertaining only to the divinity. For Jung, "that of the hidden God within."

PATTERNS OF THE ARCHETYPE

As used here (Hill) to indicate the movement of the psyche from the major constellations of the animus/anima dynamic through the polarities of the Static Feminine, Dynamic Masculine, Static Masculine and Dynamic Feminine.

PERSONA

(Latin "actor's mask) One's social role, derived from the expectations of society and early training. A strong ego relates to the outside world through a flexible persona; identification with a specific persona (doctor, scholar, career, etc.) inhibits psycholog-ical development.

PROJECTION

The process whereby an unconscious quality or charac-teristic of one's own is perceived and reacted to in an outer object or person. Applies to both negative and positive attributes.

PSYCHOANALYSIS

The formal study and application of Freud's idea of the function and develop-mental evolution of the conscious and unconscious processes of the mind through the management of the dynamic of the transference onto the ana-lyst by the patient.

PUER AETERNUS

(Latin "eternal youth") Indicates a certain type of man who remains too long in adolescent psychology, generally associated with a strong uncon-scious attachment to the mother. Counterpart is the "Puella," an "eternal girl" who remains attached to the father's world.

SELF

The archetype of wholeness and the regulating center of the personality. It is experienced as a transpersonal power (Power Greater Than One's Self) which transcends the ego, e.g. "God."

SENEX

(Latin 'old man') Associated with attitudes that come with advancing age. In the well-balanced personality functions appropriately within the puer-senex polarity.

SENSATION

One of the four "Functions" of the psyche regarded by Jung as non-rational, along with intuition, as contrasted with rational thinking/feeling.

SHADOW

An unconscious part of the personality characterized by traits and attitudes, whether negative or positive, which the conscious ego tends to reject or ignore

The inferior part of the personality; sum of all personal and collective psychic elements which, because of their incompatibility with the chosen conscious attitude, are denied expression in life and therefore coalesce into a relatively autonomous "splinter personality" with contrary tendencies in the unconscious. The shadow behaves compensatorily to consciousness; hence its effects can be positive as well as negative. In dreams, the shadow figure is always of the same sex as the dreamer.

SOUL

C. G. JUNG: "If the human (soul) is anything, it must be of unimaginable complexity and diversity, so that it cannot possibly be approached through a mere psychology of instinct. I can only gaze with wonder and awe at the depths and heights of our psychic nature. Its non-spatial universe conceals an untold abundance of Images which have accumulated over millions of years of living development and become fixed in the organism. My consciousness is like an eye that penetrates to the most distant spaces, yet it is the psychic non-ego that fills them with nonspatial images. And these images are not pale shadows, but tremendously powerful psychic factors....Beside this picture I would like to place the spectacle of the starry heavens at night, for the only equivalent of the universe within is the universe without; and just as I reach this world through the medium of the body, so I reach that world through the medium of the psyche."

SYNCHRONICITY

A term coined by Jung to designate the meaningful coincidence or equivalence (a) of a psychic and physical state or event which have no causal relationship to one another. Such synchronistic phenomena occur, for instance, when an inwardly perceived event (dream, vision, premonition, etc.) is seen to have a correspondence in external reality: the inner image of premonition has "come true"; (b) of similar or identical thoughts, dreams, etc. occurring at the same time in different places. Neither the one nor the other coincidence can be explained by causality, but seems to be connected primarily with activated archetypal processes in the unconscious.

UNCONSCIOUS, THE

That aspect of reality that is not available to consciousness. It is not just below the surface of consciousness (i.e. subconscious) but is quite literally unknown. However unknown it may be, the unconscious acts upon the individual collectively; we share a common unconscious that influences the whole of the universe.

The Collected Works of C.G. Jung

Psychiatric Studies (1902-1906)

Experimental Researches (1904-1910) (tr. Leopold Stein in collaboration with Diana Riviere)

The Psychogenesis of Mental Disease (1907-1914; 1919-1958)

Freud and Psychoanalysis (1906-1914; 1916-1930)

Symbols of Transformation (1911-1912; 1952)

Psychological Types (1921)

Two Essays on Analytical Psychology (1912-1928)

The Structure and Dynamics of the Psyche (1916-1952)

The Archetypes and the Collective Unconscious (1934-1955)

Aion: Researches into the Phenomenology of the Self (1951)

Civilization in Transition (1918-1959)

Psychology and religion: West and East (1932-1952

Psychology and Alchemy (1936-1944)

Alchemical Studies (1929-1945)

Mysterium Coniunctionis (1955-1956)

The Spirit in Man, Art, and Literature (1929-1941)

The Practice of Psychotherapy (1921-1951)

The Development of Personality (1910; 1925-1943)

The Symbolic Life: Miscellaneous Writings

General Bibliography of C.G. Jung's Writings

General Index to the Collected Works

Bibliography

Briggs-Myers, Isabel. Gifts Differing.
   1980.

Brome, Vincent. Jung Man & Myth. 1978

Carotenuto, Aldo. A Secret Symmetry
   "The Untold Story of the Woman Who
   Changed the Early History of
   Psychoanalysis." 1983.

Diller, Jerry. Freud's Jewish Identity "A
   Case Study in the Impact of Ethnicity."
   1991.

Edinger, Edward. Ego and the Archetype:
   "Individuation and the Religious
   Function of the Archetype."

Fordham, Michael. Jungian Psychotherapy.
   1978.

Frey-Rohn, Liliane. From Freud to Jung: A
   Comparative Study of the Psychology of
   the Unconscious. New York: C.G.Jung
   Foundation for Analytical Psychology,
   1974.

Gay, Peter. Freud - A Man for Our Times.
   1988.

Hall, James. A Jungian Dream
   Interpretation: A Handbook of Theory
   and Practice. Toronto: Inner City Books,
   1983.

Hannah, Barbara. Jung: His Life and Work,
   A Biographical Memoir. New York:
   Perigee Books, 1976.

Hill, Gareth. Masculine and Feminine:
   Patterns of Interaction in the Self.
   Berkeley: Shambhala, 1993.

Hopcke, Robert H. A Guided Tour of the
   Collected Works of C.G. Jung. Boston:
   Shambhala Publications, 1989.

Jacobi, Jolande. The Way of Individuation.
   1967.

Hopcke, Robert H. Jung, Jungians, and
   Homosexuality. Boston: Shambhala,
   1989.

Jacobi, Jolande. The Psychology of C.G.
   Jung. New Haven: Yale University Press,
   1973.

Jaffe, Angela. C.G. Jung Word and Image. Bollingen Series. Princeton University Press, 1979

Jung, C.G., with Jaffe, Angela. Memories, Dreams, Reflections. New York: Vintage Books, 1965.

Kerr, John. A Most Dangerous Method. 1994.

Kiersey, David and Bates, Marilyn. Please Understand Me. 1987.

MacGregor, John. The Art of the Insane. Princeton University Press, 1989.

Maidenbaum, Aryeh and Martin, Stephen A., editors. Lingering Shadows "Jungians, Freudians, and Anti-Semitism," A CG Jung Foundation Book. 1991.

McGuire, William, ed. The Freud/Jung Letters: The Correspondence between Sigmund Freud and C.G. Jung. Princeton: Princeton University Press, 1954.

Neumann, Erich. The Origins and History of Consciousness. Princeton: Princeton University Press, 1954.

Neumann, Erich. Art and the Creative Unconscious. 1959.

Nichols, Sallie. Jung and the Tarot "An Archetypal Journey," 1980.

Novwen, Henri J.M. The Wounded Healer. New York: Image Books, 1970.

Progoff, Ira. Jung's Psychology and its Social Meaning. 1973.

Segalles, Stephen and Merger, Merril. The Wisdom of the Dream. A CG Jung Foundation Book. 1990.

Singer, June. Boundaries of the Soul. New York: Doubleday, 1972.

Singer, June. Androgyny, The Opposites Within. New York: Sigo Press, 1989.

Schutz, Duane. Intimate Friends, Dangerous Rivals "The Turbulent Relationship Between Freud and Jung." 1990.

Stein, Murray, ed. Jungian Analysis. Boston & London: Shambhala, 1985.

Sulloway, Frank. Freud, Biologist of the Mind. Harvard, 1992.

Von Franz, Marie-Louise. C.G.Jung: His Myth in Our Time. New York: C.G.Jung Foundation, 1975.

Von Franz, Marie-Louise and Hillman, James. Jung's Typology. 1979.

Wehr, Gerhard. Jung: A Biography. Boston & Shaftesbury: Shambhala Publications, 1987.

Wehr, Gerhard. C.G. Jung. 1989.

Index

Jon Platania is a clinical and health psychologist in private practice in Berkeley. He completed his PhD at the Wright Institute and his post-doctoral training at the Psychology Center at the University of California. He is a graduate of the Psychotherapy Institute. He is an integrative analytic psychologist and a student of the mind-body relationship. He teaches yoga in Berkeley.

Joe Lee is the author and illustrator of CLOWNS FOR BEGINNERS, THE DANTE PRIMER, and DREAMS OF EVERY MAN. He is a graduate of Indiana University with a degree in history, and perhaps more importantly, from the ringling brothers, Barnum and Bailey Clown College. He presently resides in Bloomington, Indiana.

WHAT'S NEW?

THE BLACK HOLOCAUST FOR BEGINNERS

By S.E. Anderson; Illustrated by the Cro-maat Collective and Vanessa Holley

The Black Holocaust, a travesty that killed no less than 50 million African human beings, is the most underreported major event in world history. But it won't be for long. *The Black Holocaust For Beginners* — part indisputably documented chronicle, part passionately engaging narrative, will put this tragic event in plain sight where it belongs!
Trade paper, $11.00 ($15.75 Can., £6.99 UK), ISBN 0-86316-178-2

JAZZ FOR BEGINNERS

By Ron David; Illustrated by Vanessa Holley

An amazingly thorough guide to Jazz that is as full of blood, guts and humor as the music it describes.
Trade paper, $11.00 ($15.75 Can., £6.99 UK), ISBN 0-86316-165-0

BLACK PANTHERS FOR BEGINNERS

By Herb Boyd; Illustrated by Lance Tooks

The late 1960s, when the Panthers captured the imagination of the nation's youth, was a time of revolution. While their furious passage was marked by death, destruction, and government sabotage, the Panthers left an instructive legacy for anyone who dares to challenge the system. But don't settle for half-truths or fictionalized accounts. Learn the whole story, the way it really happened, by American Book Award winner Herb Boyd.
Trade paper, $11.00 ($15.75 Can., £6.99 UK), ISBN 0-86316-196-0

DOMESTIC VIOLENCE FOR BEGINNERS

By Alisa Del Tufo; Illustrated by Barbara Henry

Why do men hurt women — and why has so little been done about it? What can be done? A no-holds barred look at the causes and effects of spousal abuse — an epidemic by any standards that is still ignored. This book is not a luxury; it should be part of a survival kit given to everyone who buys a Marriage License. Your life — or your child's life — could depend on it.
Trade paper, $11.00 ($15.75 Can., £6.99 UK), ISBN 0-86316-1173-1

Writers and Readers

WRITERS AND READERS PUBLISHING, INC.
625 Broadway, New York, NY 10012

To order, or for a free catalog, please call (212) 982-3158; fax (212) 777-4924. MC/Visa accepted.

151

ACCEPT NO

HOW TO GET GREAT THINKERS TO COME TO YOUR HOME...

To order any current titles of Writers and Readers **For Beginners**™ books, please fill out the coupon below and enclose a check made out to **Writers and Readers Publishing, Inc.** To order by phone (with Master Card or Visa), or to receive a _free catalog_ of all our **For Beginners**™ books, please call (212) 982-3158.

Price per book: $11.00

Individual Order Form   (clip out or copy complete page)

Book Title	Quantity	Amount
	Sub Total:	
N.Y. residents add 8 1/4% sales tax		
Shipping & Handling ($3.00 for the first book; $.60 for each additional book)		
	TOTAL	

Name

Address

City   **State**   **Zip Code**

Phone number (   )

MC / VISA (circle one)   Account #   **Expires**